AFOQT Exam Prep 2019-2020

A Study Guide with 800 Test Questions and Answers for the Air Force Officer Qualifying Test

Table of Contents

Chapter 7 – Math Knowledge: Geometry 131

Chapter 8 – Reading Comprehension 165

Introduction

The United States Air Force has strict standards for admitting students. Being a member of the Air Force demonstrates pride and support for your country. Among other essential jobs, your employment can include vital support for air missions or working as a pilot for medical services. Some people who have received pilot training in the Air Force have gone on to become commercial pilots for companies all over the world.

The Air Force, like every other branch of the United States military, has strict standards for admission. One of those standards is passing the Air Force Officer Qualifying Test (AFOQT).

The Air Force Officer Qualifying Test or AFOQT is one of the most important tests that the United States Air Force uses to determine which candidates have the best potential to be trained as officers. Various changes have been implemented in the test over the years, but the goal of the test remains the same. The test is designed to test the skills that a person has to handle basic functions and ideas. This includes spatial awareness, following verbal and written instructions and math knowledge, as well as reading charts and symbols. The test also includes questions regarding aviation and the sciences—two areas that are vital for people in the Air Force to understand.

This guide includes hundreds of questions that are simulations of the real test. The strategies included in this indispensable guide will help you familiarize yourself with the type of questions you can expect on the AFOQT.

Disclaimer

The information in this guide was written to be as accurate as possible. The points are organized based on what may be expected in the AFOQT exam. All questions listed here are simulations of what may be found in the AFOQT exam. Your experience may vary, but the questions are designed to help you practice for the actual exam. Be sure to follow the information in this guide carefully, but be advised that the layout of the AFOQT exam is subject to change.

The information in this guide is not a guarantee that you will be able to complete the AFOQT exam successfully. Use the information to increase your potential for success by determining what you might expect on the test and what you should study.

Chapter 1 – The Segments of the AFOQT Exam

The AFOQT exam has multiple subtests that focus on your ability to handle verbal and math questions among other factors. What is covered in the exam is similar to what you might find in the SAT or ACT exams and the score you achieve will be an indication of your proficiency and improve your chances to be accepted into a school to become an Air Force officer.

The test can take several hours to complete, and you will only be given a certain amount of time for each subtest. People in the Air Force are expected to be able to respond quickly to certain situations, and the timing of the AFOQT test is a specific test of that ability.

The following list includes all the AFOQT subtests in their approximate order. These are covered based on the number of questions that you will be asked and the amount of time you will have to answer. Be advised that some of these subtests entail very little time, so you will have to be both fast and accurate when answering the questions.

Each of these segments will be discussed in detail throughout this guide ...

1. Verbal Analogies (25 questions, 8 minutes)

Verbal analogies test how capable you are of identifying connections between words. There can be various relationships in the analogies and how words relate to one another or how different they are from one another. For instance, you will be told that Word A is to Word B as Word C is to another word that you will have to supply. You should be able to answer at least three questions every minute.

2. Mathematical Reasoning (25 questions, 29 minutes)

This subtest measures your mathematical skills—percentages, word problems, computations and general statistics—and assesses basic math and reasoning skills.

3. Word Knowledge (25 questions, 5 minutes)

This part of the exam focuses on identifying the meanings of words. Think of this as a general dictionary review of the words that you are expected to know. You will be required to fill in a blank by choosing the definition of a word or substituting in a similar word that might be used in the place of the given word.

4. Mathematical Knowledge (25 questions, 22 minutes)

The math knowledge subtest focuses on traditional high school math. You are given less than a minute to read each question. There will be many statistics-related questions as well as some geometry. The ability to recognize equations is critical.

5. Reading Comprehension (25 questions, 38 minutes)

The reading comprehension segment will require you to work with short compositions. You will review different passages and then answer questions based on the passage. These passages vary in length but you should have enough time to review all the reading materials. In addition, you will work with multiple questions for each of the passages. Among the things to note in a reading comprehension test is its structure, who it is written for, and the main points of the narrative.

6. Instrument Comprehension (25 questions, 5 minutes)

The subtest focuses on reviewing pictures of altitude indicators, magnetic compasses and other instruments found in an airplane. The test will require you to identify a plane silhouette based on the instruments and there will be an emphasis on the position of the plane versus the horizon and the compass readings that indicate the plane's various positions in flight.

7. Block Counting (30 questions, 4.5 minutes)

The block-counting test involves a review of a stack of blocks. You need to identify how many blocks are in a stack. Other questions pertaining to the layout of the blocks may also be asked. As with other subtests, you will have to answer questions as quickly as possible, spending an average of no more than nine seconds on each question. This section really focuses on your ability to concentrate.

8. Table Reading (40 questions, 7 minutes)

This subtest involves looking at different charts or tables and then answering questions based on the information provided. On average, you should spend 10.5 seconds per question. The tables often include a random series of numbers. You'll have to identify where on a table a number is located in order to answer the questions.

9. Aviation Information (20 questions, 8 minutes)

This subtest involves basic aviation terms, concepts and general aviation principles. Most types of aircraft are covered in this guide including rotary aircraft like helicopters. The aviation section assesses your knowledge of how to control and operate an aircraft. This includes airport protocol and what to do when entering an airport to service an aircraft or handle crew or cargo.

10. General Science (20 questions, 10 minutes)

General high school science concepts are covered in this part of the test including chemistry, biology and physics among other basic principles such as the periodic table. How waves are formed, including radiation waves and light waves, is another of the topics found in this subtest.

11. Situational Judgment (50 items, 35 minutes)

The situational judgment segment focuses on how to handle particular concerns that may develop in the USAF. These include situations where you interact with officers and superiors. You will be given a hypothetical situation and will be asked to decide what is an appropriate or inappropriate action. This part of the test focuses on personal judgment.

Subtests that are not Graded

The following three subtests of the AFOQT exam are not graded. The first two focus mainly on visual acuity. The third is a basic review of personality and how well you might interact with other people.

You should not feel too much pressure when taking this part of the exam. Still, you need to understand what to expect in terms of content.

12. Rotated Blocks (15 questions, 13 minutes)

The rotated blocks subtest assesses how detail-oriented you are. One thing you might notice is that some blocks are different from each other. This means there are changes in what you might see. This is different from the previous block segment in that you will focus more on studying different blocks for similarities and differences.

13. Hidden Figures (15 questions, 8 minutes)

The hidden figures subtest involves shapes that have several small shapes inside of them. You might see many squares in one large figure or other patterns. You will be asked to accurately identify the figures that you see.

14. Self-Description Inventory (220 questions, 40 minutes)

The inventory is a personality test, intended to find out about your interests, habits, etc. This is not going to influence whether or not you will be accepted into a program but it will help with noting how you might respond to particular experiences while studying to be an Air Force officer. You should not feel pressured to give any specific responses in this part of the test, although you should always answer honestly and carefully.

Remember that you will encounter hundreds of questions in this guide to help you understand what to expect in the test.

Additional Points of Note

A few additional things to note about the AFOQT:

1. The number of questions on the subtests will not differ.

Each section has the same number of questions and you must gauge your time accordingly.

2. You will have scheduled breaks during the test.

The scheduled breaks provided during the test are designed to ensure that people are not overwhelmed.

3. You will be working with a computer during the test.

The computer that you use during the test will provide you with all the visual information that you will need to analyze in order to answer questions.

4. You will be given pen and paper if necessary.

You will more than likely need a pen and paper to calculate some of the questions on the math and science subtests of the exam. There will be questions requiring various equations and formulas and you will not be allowed the use of a calculator.

Chapter 2 – The AFOQT Scores and Subtests

The grading standards for the AFOQT exam will vary based on the area of the Air Force you want to enter. Thus, as you complete the exam, you should carefully consider the particular position you are interested in.

The grading process for the AFOQT exam is complicated, as it is difficult to determine the value of each question. Some sections will be more important than others as they will be specifically relevant to work conducted while in the Air Force. The scores are based on a combination of many subjects and are weighted based on a formula that the Air Force has not revealed. However, information on what scores are needed for each subject is available. Be advised that certain aspects of the exam may be weighted a little more than others based on the subject matter and specific position you are interested in. Test takers must complete all parts of the exam; no skipping is allowed.

The composite score you attain will be listed based on the percentage of people who have a lower score than what you achieved. For instance, you might achieve a score of 60. This means that you scored better than 60 percent of people who took the test, but lower than 40 percent of others.

General Scores for Individual Aspects of the Test

Depending on how important some aspects of the test may be, you may see certain topics tested several times. Various minimal standards are used to score the subtests.

1. Verbal Score – 15

The verbal subtest determines verbal knowledge and is divided up between verbal analogies, word knowledge and reading comprehension. You must attain a verbal score of 15 or higher in order to pass this section of the test.

The verbal subtest concentrates heavily on assessing your comprehension of particular terms used in the USAF, how you interpret verbal information and how quickly you respond.

2. Quantitative Score – 10

The quantitative score involves mathematical reasoning and knowledge. Those who complete the test must achieve a score of 10 or higher on this subtest.

3. Situational Judgment

The situational judgment subtest is particularly critical for all junior USAF officers. A person will be judged based on how well he or she is capable of making various decisions.

Remember, you must think carefully about the options given and determine the best possible decision.

4. Academic Aptitude

The academic aptitude segment of the test focuses on four aspects: a combination of the verbal analogies, mathematical reasoning, word knowledge and mathematical knowledge.

5. Pilot – 25 for pilots, 10 for CSO students

This subtest, focused on math knowledge, instrument comprehension, table reading and aviation information is relevant for people who are looking to enter the USAF and train as pilots. This includes working as a Remotely Piloted Aircraft (RPA) pilot. If you are focusing on a Combat Systems Officer (CSO) position in the Air Force you will need to attain a composite score of 25 or 10. In addition, a pilot must score a combined 50 on the pilot and CSO segments.

The pilot portion concentrates on quantitative functions and how well a person can identify parameters pertaining to an aircraft's real-time operations such as identifying the altitude of a plane, general aeronautical concepts and perceptual speed.

The pilot composite is used for potential pilots alongside a Test of Basic Aviation Skills and a requisite number of flying hours in order to be accepted for training. The Pilot Candidate Selection Method score will be calculated based on your AFOQT results and these additional tests. You will need a score of 25 in this composite if you wish to be a pilot. If you want to be a navigator, the minimum is 10.

6. CSO – 25 for CSO students, 10 for pilots

This subtest, originally known as the Navigator-Technical section, focuses on word knowledge, math knowledge, block counting and table reading. General knowledge of aeronautical aspects of operation and/or being able to identify a plane's altitude is not required. Spatial ability is a must for CSO students.

In addition to a score of 25 for the CSO segment, a CSO student will need a combined pilot and CSO score of at least 50. The pilot segment is not weighted as heavily as the CSO.

7. Air Battle Manager (ABM) – 25

The Air Battle Manager or ABM part of the AFOQT exam focuses on a variety of details pertaining to aircraft in their natural states. The module concentrates on verbal analogies, word knowledge, table reading, instrument comprehension, block counting and aviation information. The subtest is a combination of some other modules that you have already read about. You will be tested on your knowledge of aeronautics, ability to identify an airplane's altitude and perceptual speed. Spatial ability and quantitative reviews are also included.

The general categories used in each of these subtests assess your ability to manage many aspects of working within the Air Force.

What Scores are Adequate?

As discussed earlier, you will have to meet the minimums scores for each section of exam. However, the specific score that you achieve in each segment will be based on general averages. Given that the standards that the USAF has set are extremely high, it's a fair assumption that you'll probably have to attain high scores throughout the test to be invited to join the USAF.

Only the top 15 percent of people who complete the exam will be accepted into the USAF.

There are five scoring tiers:

1. A pilot requires a score of 90 or greater for the best chance to be accepted. This is the highest standard used.

2. A navigator needs a score of 85 or greater.

3. The academic portion, which determines a person's ability to manage words and mathematics, requires a score of 82 or higher in most cases.

4. The verbal part of the test requires a score of 77. Although the technical subtests are weighted more heavily than the verbal segment, you must still take this section of the test as seriously as all the others.

5. The quantitative segment requires a score of 82 or greater for admission into the USAF.

A critical note: Although some aspects of the exam are weighted more heavily, all questions and all segments are important.

How to Obtain your AFOQT Score

You will have to visit the Air Force Personnel Center website to get your test results. The results should be made available about eight to 10 days after you have taken the test.

Go to the website and enter your Social Security Number, last name and the testing center number where you took the exam. The score that you receive is valid for life, although the most recent test completed will be most important. Any older tests that you took may be disregarded, especially since there is a chance you will have improved since your first try.

Chapter 3 – Verbal Analogies

The verbal analogies subtest assesses your ability to use reasoning to determine the contexts of words as they are used in sentences. This includes looking at how words relate to one another. Your ability to identify connections is critical, but this skill also helps determine how well you manage ideas and come up with new ideas quickly.

A verbal analogy question will include a few parts:

1. You will review two words that are linked and have some relationship with one another, such as whether they are alike or opposite.
2. You will then look at two other words that will be paired with the first two. The connection between those words should be similar to the one between the first two words.
3. One of the four words in the analogy will be missing. You must decide which word will fill in the blank in order to complete the full verbal analogy.

Here is a basic example:

A cow is to milk as a chicken is to:

In this question, the cow is related to milk in that the cow produces milk. You then have to decide how the chicken is related to this situation. Look at what the chicken can produce. In this case, the answer would be an egg.

In some cases, you might see only one complete pair. You might see "A cow is to milk as ..." and then four options to choose from. You would select "a chicken is to an egg" as the correct answer. The key is to review each option and figure out which is the most sensible contextually speaking..

Types of Analogies

On the subtest you will work with one of 10 different types of analogies. Each analogy style varies based on the words being used and how they are organized.

1. Part to Whole

A part to whole analogy looks at one part of something and then decides what will constitute the whole. For instance, a question could be a mouse being to a computer as an engine is to a car. The mouse and the engine are small parts of the computer and the car, respectively. In some cases, it will be the reverse, such as "A car is to an exhaust as a computer is to a modem."

2. Cause to Effect

A cause and affect analogy involves something which causes an event to occur. In this, you may say "An oven is to heat as a freezer is to cold." A reverse example of this would be "Cold is to ice as heat is to fire."

3. Source to Product

Source to product focuses on how one item produces another. You may use this to say, "A factory is to a computer as a flower is to seeds."

4. Example to Category

The example to category analogy focuses on how something that is part of a large category. An example would be "A beagle is to a dog as a British Blue is to a cat." Dogs and cats come in many breeds, such as beagles and British Blues. You will have to determine what makes certain things similar to one another based on your knowledge.

5. General to Specific

General to specific relates a general term to a specific example. A ball may be linked to football, and then a phone may be linked to a smartphone. The ball and phone are general terms for items. The football is a specific type of ball, and a smartphone is a particular type of phone.

6. Object to Function

Certain objects might have specific functions. You'll have to review the functions of these items in an analogy question. An example of this is "A car is to drive as a football is to kick." The analogy states that you drive a car and kick a football. This may also be expressed as the opposite. The key is to also consider a definitive function of an object. While it is accurate to say that you would kick a football, since that's something everyone does, it's incorrect to say that a football is something you inflate as not all footballs can be inflated.

7. User to Tool

A person uses a tool for a specific task. This may involve a person being linked to a certain item or the other way around. You may say "An artist is to a paintbrush as a baseball player is to a bat," or "A glove is to a baseball player as a palette is to an artist." Look at how the tool in question is related to the user and assess the connection between the two.

8. Numerical

Some analogies are numerical connections between numbers. An example would be "1 is to 5 as 25 is to 125." 1 is multiplied by 5 to equal 5, and 25 would be multiplied by 5 to equal 125. Another example would be "15 is to 30 what 60 is to 75," which means that each of the first numbers in each pair is increased by 15.

9. Grammatical

A grammatical connection focuses on different words that may involve certain changes and ideas. An example would be "write is to wrote as build is to built." The first word is changed from present tense to the past tense.

10. Geographic

Geographic analogies focus on where something is located. An instance would be "Little Rock is to Arkansas as Carson City is to Nevada." The analogy states that these are the capitals of these two states. An analogy like "Sacramento is to California as Cleveland is to Ohio" would be incorrect because while the states are correct, Cleveland is not the capital of Ohio.

The goal with these analogies is to determine how the words relate to each other and what type of analogy is to be used. As the next section shows, there are several strategies that you can choose from to help you when answering verbal analogies.

Section Strategies

The following strategies may be used to answer the verbal analogies in as little time as possible.

1. Rephrase the question.

Look at the question and see if you can ask it in another way. For instance, you might see "A cub is to a bear what a _____ is to a horse." You might rephrase the question by asking, "A cub will grow up to be a bear, so what will end up growing up to be a horse?" At this point, you may realize that a foal will grow to be an adult horse, so "foal" is the answer. By rephrasing the question, you are giving yourself an opportunity to determine the type of connection.

2. Determine the general keywords based on the type of analogy you are given.

A question that entails geographic locations would be a giveaway. However, you might encounter keywords that go from being very broad to extremely specific. You may also notice that there's a difference in the meanings. You will have to look carefully at those keywords to determine the correct answers.

3. Look at the parts of speech used in the analogy.

You may notice words like verbs, nouns and adjectives that may reveal a connection. An example would be an analogy such as, "A freezer is to cold as a _____ is to hot." As you realize that a noun links to an adjective, so you should realize that a noun is needed in the blank. You would choose the answer "stove" or an appropriate answer that produces heat.

4. Look at the word tense.

Notice if the words used in the analogy are in the past, present or future tense. The analogy may be "Chicken is to fried as bread is to _____." The analogy indicates a kind of cooking process. Therefore, looking at the choices available you would select "baked."

5. Review the other choices if you still are uncertain about the correct answer.

Look at whether the choices are relevant to the keywords given. Sometimes there might be a word that does not make sense among the choices. The differences in the tenses being used in the words may also be a factor.

6. See if the meanings are alike or different.

You might come across some analogies where the words involved are not relevant to one another in an obvious manner. While many analogies use words that are similar to one another in some way, this does not mean that every analogy is going to be that way. You might have to determine the opposite of certain words.

7. Consider the relationships.

The relationships in the analogies are based on specific connections (or lack thereof between the words). You might see two things that are synonyms or antonyms. You may also notice steps in a process or things that have very specific functions. Note the relationship between the two words in the completed part of the analogy. Use this to determine what the other part of the analogy is.

8. Keep tabs on the time.

You only have eight minutes to answer 25 analogy questions. Try to devote no more than 15 to 20 seconds to each analogy.

9. Build upon your vocabulary for the best results.

Many of the questions will focus on specific terms. Draw on your vocabulary to determine the meaning of different words. This applies for the word knowledge subtest as well.

Verbal Analogies Questions

1. Rein is to horse as control panel is to:
    a. Pilot
    b. Bit
    c. Plane
    d. Rider

2. Buenos Aires is to Argentina as _____ is to Canada:
    a. Ottawa
    b. Toronto
    c. Montreal
    d. Calgary

3. _____ is to lay as sing is to anthem:
    a. Act
    b. Scene
    c. Theater
    d. Field

4. Mouse is to computer as flash button is to:
    a. Modem
    b. Camera
    c. Phone
    d. Tablet

5. A shelf is to a bookcase as a cushion is to a:
    a. Sofa
    b. Frame
    c. Desk
    d. Table

6. Scrub is to wash as sob is to:
    a. Cry
    b. Water
    c. Sad
    d. Tease

7. Moisten is to _____ as cool is to freeze:
    a. Water
    b. Soak
    c. Oven
    d. Grow

8. Togetherness is to unity as _____ is to scarcity:
    a. Abundance
    b. Link
    c. Connection
    d. Lack

9. A bowling alley is to a lane as a golf course is to a:
    a. Ball
    b. Club
    c. Court
    d. Hole

10. A nail is to wood as a staple is to:
    a. Paper
    b. Concrete
    c. Clay
    d. Grass

11. A dolphin is to a pod as a cow is to a:
    a. Herd
    b. Gaggle
    c. Flock
    d. Field

12. To reduce is to decrease as _____ is to increase:
    a. Enhance
    b. Add
    c. Bring up
    d. Arrange

13. An urn is to ashes as a wallet is to:
    a. Money
    b. Values
    c. Paper
    d. Belief

14. Doze is to sleep as sneak is to:
    a. Run
    b. Crawl
    c. Walk
    d. Stay idle

15. To approach is to _____ as to leave is to bolt:
    a. Enter
    b. Pounce
    c. Require
    d. Rain

16. An orange is to Florida as a pineapple is to:
    a. Washington
    b. California
    c. Arizona
    d. Hawaii

17. To search is to find as to attack is to:
    a. Defeat
    b. Reduce
    c. Cross
    d. Discover

18. A quarry is to marble as a hive is to:
    a. Bees
    b. Trees
    c. Honey
    d. Sugar

19. A ribbon is to a _____ as icing is to a cake:
    a. Decoration
    b. Present
    c. Label
    d. Tie

20. An invoice is to money as a diary is to:
    a. Observations
    b. Letters
    c. Requests
    d. Debts

21. A pharaoh is to Egypt as an emperor is to:
    a. Rome
    b. Madrid
    c. Baghdad
    d. Cairo

22. A top hat is to Monopoly as a _____ is to chess:
    a. Board
    b. Rook
    c. Timer
    d. Game advantage

23. A kitten is to a litter as a soldier is to an:
    a. Army
    b. Entity
    c. Location
    d. Base

24. A bracelet is to a wrist as a _____ is to a waist:
    a. Anklet
    b. Belt
    c. Shoe
    d. Headband

25. A shark is to the ocean as a bald eagle is to:
    a. The air
    b. The land
    c. Underground areas
    d. Trees

26. Algebra is to calculus as _____ is to surgery:
    a. Anatomy
    b. Doctor
    c. Hospital
    d. Knife

27. A scientist is to an experiment as an actor is to a:
    a. Play
    b. Game
    c. Concert
    d. Test

28. A dove is to peace as a lion is to:
    a. Excitement
    b. War
    c. Courage
    d. Fear

29. A serve is to tennis as a _____ is to golf:
    a. Putt
    b. Chip
    c. Save
    d. Tee shot

30. A tooth is to a _____ as a tine is to a fork:
    a. Knife
    b. Mouth
    c. Tongue
    d. Comb

31. A grove is to a forest as a _____ is to a lake:
    a. Boat
    b. Tree
    c. Pond
    d. Ocean

32. A shower is to a deluge as a glance is to a:
    a. Peek
    b. Look
    c. Review
    d. Stare

33. Coffee is to a mug as soup is to a:
    a. Bowl
    b. Saucer
    c. Plate
    d. Meal

34. An ax is to chop as a _____ is to cut:
    a. Tree
    b. Saw
    c. Shovel
    d. Rail

35. Irrelevant is to significant as asleep is to:
    a. Awake
    b. Calm
    c. Restful
    d. Thoughtful

36. A carousel is to luggage as an elevator is to:
    a. Crates
    b. People
    c. Vehicles
    d. Shipments

37. A road is to a highway as a net is to a _____:
    a. Court
    b. Lane
    c. Park
    d. Median

38. Batter is to a pancake as dough is to:
    a. Bread
    b. Cake
    c. Yeast
    d. Flour

39. A visor is to a hat as a collar is to a:
    a. Pant
    b. Hood
    c. Sweater
    d. Shirt

40. A goal is to ice hockey as a _____ is to gridiron football:
    a. Touchdown
    b. Field goal
    c. Safety
    d. Extra point

41. An omelet is to dinner as a _____ is to breakfast:
    a. Pancake
    b. Doughnut
    c. Steak
    d. Cereal

42. To _____ is to product butter as to press is to produce wine:
    a. Steam
    b. Heat
    c. Freeze
    d. Churn

43. A crumb is to bread as an _____ is to a molecule:
    a. Atom
    b. Ion
    c. Helix
    d. Shred

44. A sheath is to a knife as a holster is to a:
    a. Pistol
    b. Club
    c. Grenade
    d. Mine

45. Innovation is to tradition as _____ is to custom.
    a. Standard
    b. Regulation
    c. Thrill
    d. Surprise

46. To cancel is to delay as to surrender is to:
    a. Yield
    b. Continue
    c. Forgive
    d. Stop

47. A deck is to a ship as a _____ is to a plane:
    a. Cockpit
    b. Control center
    c. Dock
    d. Surface

48. Thrifty is to reckless as _____ is to hurried:
    a. Sensible
    b. Quick
    c. Fast
    d. Patient

49. To dominate is to conquer as to celebrate is to:
    a. Party
    b. Attain
    c. Lead
    d. Achieve

50. A dessert is to a meal as an _____ is to a novel:
    a. Conclusion
    b. Epilogue
    c. Appendix
    d. Index

51. A _____ is to a property as to plagiarize entails with words:
    a. Willing
    b. Sports
    c. Poaching
    d. Crossword

52. A speech is to a _____ as a race is to a track:
    a. Preamble
    b. Tote
    c. Lectern
    d. Odds

53. A _____ is to a flood as a helmet is to an injury:
    a. Levee
    b. River
    c. Float
    d. Boat

54. A _____ is to a team as a freshman is to a college:
    a. Junior
    b. Rookie
    c. Player
    d. Senator

55. A _____ is to a bi

    a. Bond
    b. Charges
    c. Foot
    d. Doctor

56. To be potable is   ₅:

    a. Navigable
    b. Portable
    c. Drinking
    d. Potting

57. A _____ is to a channel as a flare is to an accident:

    a. Buoy
    b. River
    c. Television set
    d. Design

58. A slight is to hurt as a lag is to:

    a. Being late
    b. Haste
    c. Heft
    d. Bragging

59. A fist is to a hand as a _____ is to a loop:

    a. Foot
    b. Circuit
    c. Wave
    d. Ring

60. A bonsai is to a _____ as a sequoia is to a forest:

    a. Sunshine
    b. Leaf
    c. Pot
    d. Garden

61. Television is to screen as a computer is to _____:

    a. Monitor
    b. Label
    c. Cord
    d. Link

62. Pencil is to lead as pen is to _____:
     a. Graphite
     b. Ink
     c. Clay
     d. Rubber

63. Fire is to ice as break is to _____:
     a. Fracture
     b. Build
     c. Bend
     d. Strengthen

64. Yield is to triangle as _____ is to octagon:
     a. One way
     b. Stop
     c. Wrong way
     d. Crossing

65. Cut is to scissors as _____ is to blower:
     a. Dry
     b. Comb
     c. Edge
     d. Straighten

66. The sun is to clouds as the moon is to _____:
     a. Stars
     b. Air
     c. Wind
     d. Light

67. Fire is to scorch as ice is to _____:
     a. Freeze
     b. Stop
     c. Melt
     d. Wear

68. Finger is to _____ as toe is to foot:
     a. Leg
     b. Wrist
     c. Hand
     d. Ankle

69. Gun is to shoot as bomb is to:
    a. Explode
    b. Light
    c. Round
    d. Detonate

70. Lift is to weight as drain is to:
    a. Water
    b. Pressure
    c. Mass
    d. Stone

71. Paint is to an easel as a chisel is to a:
    a. Rock
    b. Clay surface
    c. Attachment
    d. Link

72. An officer is to a manager as a school is to a:
    a. Teacher
    b. Custodian
    c. Counselor
    d. Principal

73. A spoon is to stir as a knife is to:
    a. Poke
    b. Cut
    c. Blend
    d. Mix

74. A dictionary is to definitions as a _____ is to synonyms:
    a. Thesaurus
    b. Almanac
    c. Guidebook
    d. Reference list

75. Columbus is to Ohio as _____ is to Nevada:
    a. Las Vegas
    b. Reno
    c. Carson City
    d. Mesquite

76. Drum is to instrument as a drill is to:
    a. Hammer
    b. Oven
    c. Tool
    d. Climax

77. Sheet is to pad as a flower is to:
    a. Bouquet
    b. Card
    c. Plant
    d. Surface

78. _____ is to real as hostile is to friendly:
    a. Fake
    b. Authentic
    c. True
    d. Very

79. Pilgrim is to _____ as a recluse is to home:
    a. Space
    b. Ocean
    c. Journey
    d. Tour

80. A is to alternating as D is to:
    a. Direct
    b. Dynamic
    c. Divided
    d. Diverse

81. Brownies are to cocoa as an omelet is to:
    a. Cheese
    b. Milk
    c. Pancake
    d. Egg

82. Query is to question as queue is to:
    a. Quiz
    b. Layout
    c. Surprise
    d. Line

83. Amplify is to enhance as abate is to:
  a. Multiply
  b. Divide
  c. Reduce
  d. Plan

84. Astronomer is to space as a spelunker is to:
  a. Water
  b. Cave
  c. Light
  d. Forest

85. Quick is to slow as youth is to:
  a. Elderly
  b. Simple
  c. Immature
  d. Adult

86. Baseball is to throw as puck is to:
  a. Kick
  b. Shoot
  c. Dribble
  d. Whip

87. Horse is to gallop as rabbit is to:
  a. Crawl
  b. Hop
  c. Prance
  d. Tire

88. A tree is to sap as a hydrant is to:
  a. Water
  b. Juice
  c. Soap
  d. Heat

89. An octagon is to 8 as a _____ is to 6:
  a. Pentagon
  b. Hexagon
  c. Decagon
  d. Polygon

90. A ruler is to length as a protractor is to:
    a. Size
    b. Angle
    c. Distance
    d. Mass

91. A mastiff is to dog as a thresher is to:
    a. Cattle
    b. Cat
    c. Pig
    d. Bird

92. Rigid is to flexible as _____ is to clear:
    a. Confident
    b. Understandable
    c. Right
    d. Fuzzy

93. Slither is to snake as _____ is to fan.
    a. Revolve
    b. Accelerate
    c. Rotate
    d. Speed

94. 5 is to 4 as 8 is to:
    a. 6
    b. 7
    c. 9
    d. 10

95. 2 million is to 2 billion as 1 thousand is to:
    a. 1 million
    b. 1 hundred thousand
    c. 1 billion
    d. 1 hundred

96. Liberia is to Africa as _____ is to South America.
    a. Argentina
    b. Guatemala
    c. New Zealand
    d. Tunisia

97. To begin is to commence as to end is to:
   a. Move
   b. Plan
   c. Cease
   d. Argue

98. A sari is to India as a _____ is to Scotland:
   a. Kimono
   b. Kilt
   c. Sarong
   d. Serape

99. A mustang is to a horse as a _____ is to a cat:
   a. Camino
   b. Jaguar
   c. Pelican
   d. Panther

100.   Dickens is to a novel as Dickenson is to a:
   a. Epic
   b. Poem
   c. Play
   d. Song

Verbal Analogies Answers

1. c. The control panel controls the plane while a rein controls a horse.
2. a. Buenos Aires is the capital of Argentina, Ottawa is the capital of Canada.
3. a. A person will act in a play, and someone will sing an anthem.
4. b. The flash button is used on a camera for taking pictures. The mouse would be used on the computer for clicking to active certain things.
5. a. The cushion makes up a small part of a sofa, while a shelf makes up a portion of a bookcase.
6. a. Scrubbing is intense washing, and sobbing is extreme crying.
7. b. A small bit of water added to something moistens it. However, when you add more water, the item is soaked. This can be said for cooling items, in that something that is cooled is treated lightly, but something that is cooled to the extreme will freeze.
8. The pairs are synonyms. Togetherness and unity are the same, and scarcity is a lack of something.
9. d. A hole is one part of a golf course, and a lane is one part of a bowling alley.
10. a. A staple will attach sheets of paper together. A nail will secure pieces of wood together.
11. a. A group of cattle is a herd, while a group of dolphins is a pod.
12. b. Synonyms add and increase are the same and reduces and decreases are also the same.
13. a. While a loved one's ashes are in an urn after cremation, a person's money is in a wallet.
14. a. This refers to polar opposites of the same kind. A doze is not sleeping completely, but it can lead to sleep. Sneaking is going slowly, but it could lead to running.

15. b. An arrival can take a bit of time; a pounce is an arrival that occurs all of a sudden. A person may also take some time to leave, but that someone can also bolt and leave suddenly.

16. d. The analogy is fruits based on in what states they are grown. While oranges can be found throughout Florida, pineapples can be found in Hawaii.

17. a. The analogy is the possible end results. While a search will result in someone finding things, an attack will result in a person defeating an opponent.

18. c. A quarry is a place where marble can be mined. A hive is a place where honey can be gathered.

19. b. A present can be decorated with a ribbon. A cake may be decorating with icing.

20. a. A diary will include many observations that a person might write. An invoice will include details of the money that a person is owed.

21. a. A pharaoh would be someone who would have ruled ancient Egypt; an emperor is someone who would have ruled the ancient city of Rome.

22. b. A rook is one of the pieces that you can use when playing chess. A top hat is one of the pieces that you could use when playing the board game Monopoly.

23. a. An army will have many soldiers, and a litter will have many kittens.

24. b. A belt is worn around a waist like a bracelet is worn around a wrist.

25. a. A shark can be seen swimming in the ocean; a bald eagle can be seen flying in the air.

26. a. A person who wishes to study calculus must be successful in studying algebra. A person who wants to work in a surgical field must understand anatomy.

27. a. A scientist will take part in an experiment, and an actor will take part in a play.

28. c. A lion is often symbolic of courage, and a dove is a symbol of peace.

29. d. The serve is the first move that occurs in a tennis competition. For a golf round, the tee shot is the first thing that will take place.

30. d. A comb features many teeth that combine to produce a functional item. A fork includes a series of tines that produce something useful for eating.

31. c. A grove is a smaller version of a forest. A pond is a small lake.

32. d. A deluge occurs when a shower becomes intense. A stare is like a glance, except the stare lasts much longer and provides an intense look.

33. a. Soup is to be poured into a bowl just as coffee can be poured into a mug.

34. b. A saw being used to cut materials and an ax chops things.

35. a. The 2 points refer to antonyms. A person is awake and is the opposite of being asleep, and something that is significant is the opposite of irrelevant.

36. b. An elevator will carry people to different places like a baggage carousel at an airport moves luggage from one place to another.

37. a. A net is a small part of a court, and a road is one part of a larger highway.

38. a. The end products of batter and dough are pancakes and bread respectively.

39. d. The collar is a small part of a shirt just as a visor is a part of a hat.

40. a. The main goal of playing ice hockey is to score a goal. For gridiron football, the overall goal is to score a touchdown.

41. c. This analogy refers to foods that are consumed at the opposite times of day. People are not likely to consume omelets during dinner and they would not consume steak for breakfast.

42. d. The churning process is the production of butter. This is similar to what is necessary to produce wine.

43. a. An atom is a small part of a molecule and is not necessarily complex like a double helix pattern nor does it have a charge like an ion.

44. a. The analogy considers how you would store items in certain things.

45. d. The analogy is how certain things are opposite to one another. A surprise will happen differently than a custom to be followed.

46. a. When a team yields, that team will start to ease up, but it will not necessarily surrender. This is similar to what happens when something is delayed. The event is not canceled, but it is not necessarily going as planned.

47. a. The cockpit is a space where the plane is to be controlled.

48. d. A thrifty person would be careful about spending and would be anything but reckless.

49. a. A party occurs when one celebrates things, just like conquering occurs following domination.

50. b. The epilogue appears as the conclusion to a narrative novel. A conclusion would be for a report, while an appendix would be any additional bits of information that would support whatever had been introduced.

51. c. Poaching refers to taking something that belongs to someone else. In this analogy, a person may poach a property and try to use it for one's own advantage.

52. c. A speech will occur at a lectern, and a race occurs on a track.

53. a. A levee will prevent a flood from occurring, and a helmet prevents injury.

54. b. While a freshman is new to a college, a rookie is new to a team.

55. c. To foot a bill is to cover the charges. This is similar to how reimbursements cover expenses.

56. c. When something is potable, that means it can be drunk safely.

57. a. A buoy and a flare can both be used to mark things and a channel and the site of an accident on a road marks the place.

58. a. A lag is someone being late for something.

59. b. A circuit will work as a part of a loop, particularly within a connection. This is similar to how a fist works as part of a hand.

60. c. A large sequoia tree can be found in a forest, a smaller bonsai tree would be small enough to be planted in a pot.

61. a. The monitor in this refers to the thing that a person is using to view. The monitor is on the computer, while people view a television using a screen.

62. b. A pencil may use a form of lead, while a pen will use some kind of ink.

63. c. The analogies are opposite actions. Fire is the opposite of ice, and bending is the opposite of breaking when something experiences pressure.

64. b. A yield sign is shaped like a triangle, while a stop sign is an octagon.

65. a. A pair of scissors will help cut hair, while a blower will dry the hair.

66. a. The sun is likely to be surrounded by clouds in a typical day. The moon would be surrounded by stars at night.

67. a. Fire scorches surfaces, while ice freezes.

68. c. The toe refers to the foot and not to the ankle.

69. d. You would shoot a gun, and you would detonate a bomb.

70. a. You may lift weights, but you may drain water from a surface.

71. a. While you would add paint to an easel, a chisel would be used on a rock surface to produce a sculpture.

72. d. A principal is the leading authority at a school, and a manager is a leading authority at an office.

73. b. You would use a knife to cut things like you would do when stirring something with a spoon.

74. a. A thesaurus includes information on synonyms.

75. c. Columbus is the capital of Ohio; Carson City is the capital of Nevada.

76. c. A drum is an instrument, and a drill would work as a tool.

77. a. A single flower may be part of a larger bouquet, and a single sheet of paper may be a part of a much larger pad.

78. While hostile is the opposite of friendly, fake is the opposite of real.

79. A recluse would stay at home, while a pilgrim is someone who would go on a far-off journey to another place.

80. a. AC refers to alternating current, while DC is the direct current.

81. d. The egg is critical to the product of an omelet, just as cocoa is critical in making brownies.

82. d. A queue is another word for a line, and a query is another word for a question.

83. c. To abate is to reduce something's intensity.

84. b. While an astronomer explores space, a spelunker explores a cave.

85. a. This analogy is polar opposites. An elderly person is the opposite of someone who is much younger.

86. b. The analogy involves what people do with sporting items. A person might pitch a baseball, and a hockey player would shoot a puck.

87. b. The ways these animals would move is this analogy. A rabbit hops, and a horse gallops.

88. A hydrant includes an extensive amount of water, while a tree contains lots of sap on the inside.

89. b. A hexagon has 6 sides and an octagon has 8.

90. b. A protractor is a tool used to measure the angles on different items.

91. d. A thresher is a type of bird and a mastiff is a breed of dog.

92. d. Being fuzzy is the opposite of clear.

93. c. A fan may rotate as it moves to produce air.

94. c. Adding one to each part of the analogy.

95. a. Three zeroes are added to the end of either one.

96. a. Liberia is a country in Africa, and Argentina is a country in South America.
97. c. You commence something at the start and then cease when you are done.
98. b. The analogy covers traditional clothing items that are found in different countries.
99. b. The mustang and jaguar are both animals that belong to specific animal families.
100. b. Charles Dickens is known for writing novels, and Emily Dickinson is known for writing   poems.

Chapter 4 – Math Reasoning

Mathematics is one of the most important subjects used in the Air Force. Therefore, it is no surprise that the subtest on mathematical reasoning is particularly critical.

The mathematical reasoning subtest focuses on many standard mathematical concepts. Many of the questions on this part of the test are simple relationships between numbers.

This chapter focuses on identifying the particular things you may notice when working on this part of the AFOQT exam. This includes a review of the types of math equations and problems you will have to solve, to include fractions and exponents among many other concepts.

Note: You will not be able to use a calculator on the AFOQT exam. The general mathematical reasoning subtest is typically different from the math knowledge section. Additional details on the math knowledge subtest, particularly pertaining to algebra and geometry, will be covered in a later chapter in this guide.

The questions are all multiple choice, so you can eliminate certain answers that you automatically know are incorrect.

Properties and Types of Integers

The number of questions you will encounter for each aspect of the mathematical reasoning test will vary based on the test you are given.

1. Basic Mathematical Operations

General math operations are: add, subtract, multiply or divide numbers. Sometimes you may find some questions that are straightforward, like 345 + 146. In other cases, you might deal with more complicated questions. An example would be, "If Jeff runs 3 miles a day, 5 days a week, how many weeks would be required for him to run past the 26.2-mile marker?" You have to calculate how many 15-mile weeks are required to get to that mile marker. Your answers should be 1.746 weeks.

2. Divisibility

Divisibility means to divide numbers. The number that is subject to division is called the dividend and the number used to divide into the dividend is called the divisor. The result of the division (answer) is called the quotient. For example, 455 can be divided by various numbers. You could divide 455 by 5, 7 or 13, but 455 is not divisible evenly by 9, 11 or 15.

Divisibility is also a factor when working with fractions. Fractions are division problems: the numerator is divided by the denominator. You will always need to reduce a fraction to its lowest form. An example is the fraction 16/30, which should be reduced to 8/15.

3. Prime Numbers

A prime number cannot be divided by any number other than itself and 1. Such numbers include 2, 3, 5, 7, 19, 71 and 89 among countless others.

4. Multiples and Squares

Multiples are produced when a number is multiplied by an integer rather than a fraction. For instance, 27 is a multiple of 3 and 55 is a multiple of 11.

A number squared is the integer multiplied by itself. For example, 9 is the square of 3; 16 is the square of 4; 36 is the square of 6; 324 is a square of 18 and so forth.

5. Remainders

A remainder is what is left over when a divisor does not divide evenly into a dividend. You might encounter a question such as finding the remainder of 45 divided by 6.

6. Odd and Even Integers

While integers are basic numbers, they may be either positive or negative. Such integers should be noted as whole numbers, as any number with a decimal or fraction is not an integer. You might be asked to find the next number in the sequence of 2, 4, 8, 14, 22. As each number is increased by 2 and then 4 and then 6 and so forth, the next number would be 32.

7. Exponents and Roots

An exponent refers to a quantity for the number to be raised to a certain power. That is, the number is multiplied by itself a few times. In many cases, you might come across a question like 2^3, which is 2 multiplied by itself 3 times; or 4^4, which is 4 multiplied by itself 4 times.

Roots determine how a certain number may be divisible by a whole number. This is the reverse of exponents in that you're looking at a larger number and figuring out what number is to be multiplied by itself to get that number. The root of 81 is 9, and the root of 144 is 12.

8. Whole Numbers and Decimals

A whole number is a number that does not include a decimal. For instance, 2 and 3 are whole numbers; 2.15 and 3.634 are not whole numbers, as they are decimals.

9. Fractions

Fractions are two numbers that, when divided, will produce decimals. The top number is the numerator, while the bottom number is the denominator. Therefore, for the fraction 7/8, 7 is the numerator and 8 is the denominator.

10. Rational and Irrational Numbers

A rational number is a number that can be listed as a fraction. For instance, 15/5 is a rational number in that it stands for the number 3; 14/8 is also rational as it equals 1.75. A number represented as π or 22/7 is an irrational number, as it equals 3.141592 ... The decimal continues to infinity.

General Concepts

It's very likely that you'll come across questions involving many of the following concepts:

1. Estimation

Estimation helps you quickly determine approximate answers. This is for cases where you have large numbers to work with or many calculations to perform.

2. Percent

Percent involves multiplication and division. For example, 80% is 80 divided by 100 and is represented by 80/100. When calculating 80% of 60, the calculation is 80/100 multiplied by 60, which is 48.

3. Ratio

You might be given a ratio of 2:1 ratio, for example. This means that two of one number appears for every one of the other. In other words, the first number is twice the second.

4. Rate

A rate can refer to a percentage. This could include a number increasing at a particular rate, such as every hour. This could include a plane traveling in the air at a certain rate, or increasing or decreasing by a certain speed every hour. Rate is also used to calculate interest to be paid over a certain length of time.

5. Absolute Value

The absolute value of something is the general magnitude of a real number without concern for its sign. One thing to note here is that with an absolute number, the total may be a positive integer. For instance, an absolute number $|x|$ may equal x if it is positive. The absolute number $|x|$ would equal $-x$ if the original x value is a negative amount and $|0|$ would continue to remain as 0 regardless. For instance, the absolute value of 2 remains 2, and the absolute value of -2 may also be 2.

6. The Number Line

Traditionally used when comparing real numbers to others, a number line is a series of real numbers organized in a straight line, spaced evenly from one another. A line may include numbers like 1, 2 and 3, or it could have a sequence like 3, 6 and 9. The number of integers in between each space will be equal depending on the number line.

7. Decimal Representation

The decimal representation point refers to where a decimal point is going to go when working on particular numbers in equations. In many cases, decimal representation will be reflective of percentages of division-related problems. For instance, 73% is 73/100 which equals 73.

8. Number Sequences

A number sequence refers to how numbers in a number line relate to one another. For instance, in a number sequence of 5, 11, 17, 23 and 29, 35 would be next number because 6 has been added to each of the previous numbers. The number sequence of 20, 23, 27 and 32 would have 38 as its next number because 3 is added to the first number and 4 is added to the next—the number added to each in that sequence will increase by one.

The Base-10 Number System

The base-10 system, also referred to as a decimal system, is the process used for placing values on numerals. Value is determined by where a digit is when compared with the decimal points.

Every integer is 10 times the value of the number that is to the immediate right. A number that is greater than 1 will have any values that appear to the left of a decimal point. These numbers have the following values (the 1 in each of these examples refers to the placement of the number in a certain value):

1 – ones

10 – tens

100 – hundreds

1,000 – thousands

10,000 – 10 thousands

100,000 – hundred thousands

1,000,000 – millions

Any value that is a fraction or which has a value that is less than 1 will have places that appear to the right of the decimal point.

.1 – tenths

.01 – hundredths

.001 – thousandths

.0001 – 10 thousandths

.00001 – hundred thousandths

.000001 – millionths

For instance, you might be asked which digit in .34621 is in the thousandths position. The correct answer to that question is 6.

Or you might be given the number 514,382.769. Note that 5 is in the hundred-thousand position and has a value of 500,000 in this question; 3 is in the hundreds position with a value of 300; 9 is in the thousandths space with a value of 9/1000.

One related aspect of base-10 values is the concept of rounding. There are times when you might have to round a number to a certain position. For instance, you may be asked to round 543,686 to the nearest thousandth, meaning the answer is 544,000. Or, if you asked to round 3,342.684 to the nearest hundredth, the answer would be 3,342.68.

The Factor Tree

The factor tree is a representation of a larger number broken down into its components. Here is an example:

$$42$$

$$/ \qquad \backslash$$

$$6 \qquad 7$$

$$/ \quad \backslash \qquad \backslash$$

2 3   7

In this factor tree, 42 is the product of 6 and 7; and 6 is the product of 2 and 3. You cannot factor 7 any further, as that is a prime number ...

There are other ways that the same factor tree could be represented. For example:

```
                    42
        /                    \
        2                    21
   /    \                      \
   2    3                      7
```

Math Operations

1. General Numerical Layout

You will have to complete various operations on this part of the AFOQT exam, often pertaining to how numbers are arranged with one another. In some cases, you will have to solve a question by arranging the numbers in columns. That is, one number will be on top of the other depending on the action that will take place. For instance, 345 + 615 would become:

345

+615

You could use this vertical layout to help you with adding, subtracting or performing other calculations.

2. Order of Solving

Any math problems you solve on the AFOQT exam must be solved in order. The PEMDAS acronym can be used to identify the order to follow when calculating operations: Parentheses, Exponents, Multiplication, Division, Addition and Subtraction. Whatever is in parentheses is calculated first, exponents are second, etc.

For example:

$3 + 4(6 \times 5)$

In this case, you would have to multiply the 6x5 first, which equals 30. Next, calculate 3 plus 4, which equals 7. Now you have 7 times 30, which equals 210.

Next are the exponents. For example:

$34 + 4^3$

For this question, you would calculate the number with the exponent first: 4^3 or 4 x 4 x 4, which equals 64. Then add 34 and 64, which equals 98.

3. Fractions

On the test you may have to add, subtract or multiply fractions. You should be aware of both numerators and denominators. This is because if the denominators of each fraction are the same, you only need to add the numerators. For instance, 3/8 + 4/8 would be 7/8. Conversely, if the denominators are different from one another you will have to adjust the fractions by finding a common denominator by multiplying one or both of the fractions involved. For 1/5 + 2/6, the common denominator of 5 and 6 is 30; and the problem becomes 6/30 + 10/30, which is 16/30, and reduced would become 8/15.

The same consideration can be used for when you're subtracting fractions. For example, 6/11 − 1/3. The common denominator of 11 and 3 is 33. So the fractions now are 18/33 − 11/33, which is 7/33.

Multiplication of fractions requires multiplying both the numerators and denominators. For example, for 3/5 x 6/8, multiply the numerators of 3 x 6 and the denominators of 5 x 8. This equals 18/40, which would then be reduced to 9/20.

There may be times where you have to multiply a whole number and/or add it to something else. You might be given 6 x 1/3. The equation can be expressed as (6x2) ÷ 3, which is 12 ÷ 3, which equals 4.

4. Multiple Decimal Places

You may find some questions where you have to consider different decimal places. For example, add 1.346 and 4.56.

In this example, you would add a 0 to the end of the number that has the fewest decimal places. The 4.56 would thus become a 4.560. The number should be easier for you to add to 1.346, especially since the number of decimal places is the same. After adding the numbers together, your final answer should be 5.906.

Converting Fractions, Decimals and Percentages

1. Managing Fractions

If you are given a fraction like 18/20, first reduce 18/20 to its lowest form. The numerator and denominator can be divided by 2, which equals 9/10; 16/40 could be reduced to 8/20 and reduced again to 4/10, and again to 2/5. This is a much easier way of using that fraction.

There may also be times when you can take a large fraction that is worth more than 1 and simplify it to a whole number and a fraction. For instance, 15/4 can be expressed as 3 3/4.

2. Converting Fractions to Decimals

Next, convert a fraction to a decimal by dividing the numerator by the denominator. For example, 3/4 is converted to a decimal by dividing 3 by 4, which equals .75 (decimal 75).

3. Converting Percentages

You may need to convert a percentage to a number, such as 45%. Take the hypothetical decimal point at the end of 45 and divide it by 100, which moves the decimal at the end of 45 two places to the left. This gives you 0.45 and the correct value of 45%; 75.87% would thus be 0.7587 (move the decimal two places to the left).

To convert a number to a percentage, the number is multiplied by 100, which is the same as moving the decimal two places to the right. Then add the percentage symbol. Conversely, to express 0.1478 as a percentage, move the decimal two places to the right, which is 14.78%.

You might be asked to get 45% of 85. For this, 45% is expressed as 0.45. Next, multiply.45 x 85, which is 38.25 (45% of 85 = 38.25).

Long Division

Since you do not have access to a calculator during the AFOQT exam, you will be required to use long division to arrive at answers to various math-related questions. You will have to take the dividend in an equation and divide it by the divisor. For example, in the division question of 384/5 or 384 ÷ 5; 384 is the dividend, and 5 is the divisor. This is likely something you were taught in elementary school. It's a good idea to revisit it prior to the exam.

Long Multiplication

The long multiplication process requires multiple steps, also probably taught in your elementary school.

There may be situations where you are asked to multiply numbers that have multiple decimal places. For example, 5.4 x 4.344 = 23.4576. By counting the number of decimal places in the two numbers being multiplied, you know the answer will require four decimal places.

Positive and Negative Numbers

1. Addition – Positive and Negative

You may be asked to solve something like -45 + 30. In this case, you can move the -45 to the other side of the equation to produce 30 − 45, which results in -15.

2. Addition – Two Negative Numbers

You may also be asked to add two negative numbers. For example, -50 + -40. The equation should be treated as a subtraction problem. You can convert the equation to -50 – 40. This gives you the answer of -90.

3. Subtraction – Positive and Negative

Subtracting a positive and negative number is easy if the negative number appears first and you are subtracting a number from it. If the inverse is true, you will need to cancel out the negative and subtraction parts to turn this into an addition problem. 60 - -30 would become 60 + 30, thus giving you 90. You are subtracting -30 from 60, which is the opposite of reversing the number, thus making this an addition.

4. Subtraction – Two Negative Numbers

When working with two negative numbers, you are turning the situation into a positive. For example, -12 - -11. As with the prior example, make this into an addition equation by combining the minus and second negative to create a positive. Then you add 11 to -12 to get -1 as your answer.

5. Multiplication – Positive and Negative

When you multiply a positive number with a negative one or the other way around, the product will be negative. For example, -5 x 8 gives you a product of -40.

6. Multiplication – Two Negative Numbers

Multiplying two negative numbers with one another will produce a positive answer. The question -8 x -5 equals a product of 40.

7. Division – Positive and Negative

As with multiplication, you will also get a negative answer when you divide a positive number by a negative one or the other way around. For example, -15 / 3 would equal -5, as would 15 / -3.

8. Division – Two Negative Numbers

The same thing happens when multiplying two negative numbers. Two negatives produce a positive. You can take -15 / -3 to get a result of 5.

Order and Comparison

The order and comparison uses specific symbols. These symbols are as follows:

<less than

>greater than

≤less than or equal to

≥greater than or equal to

A left-pointing arrow means a number is less than something, and a right-pointing arrow is greater than something.

Square Roots

Square roots are among the more complicated concepts on this section of the test, but it helps to understand how they're useful. A square root involves considering a number and determining what number has to be divided by itself to get the answer. For instance:

$\sqrt{36}$

What number multiplied by itself equals 36? The square root of 36 is 6, as that number multiplied by itself equals 35. In other words, $6^2 = 36$.

There are a few things that you can do when trying to determine a square root:

1. Estimate the number.

For instance, you might need to find the square root of 79. You may know from a multiplication table that the square root of 81 is 9. Therefore, you can make a guess from the choices available, selecting the closest answer to 9.

2. Divide the number by one of the square roots.

You can also divide a number by the nearest square root if you need something precise. For example, you may be asked to find the square root of 52. You could divide 52 by 7 because you know that 7 squared is 49, so you know that the answer you should choose will be more than 7 but less than 8.

Matrices

A matrix is a layout of numbers listed in rows and columns in a set of brackets. These are often used to indicate numbers that are related to each other together.

You can identify the value of a number in a matrix by looking at the row and column a number is in. You may see a variable and then two smaller numbers next to that variable. The first number is the row and the second is the column. To understand this, here is an example:

$$g = \begin{bmatrix} 4 & 5 & 6 \\ 5 & 6 & 4 \\ 3 & 2 & 7 \end{bmatrix}$$

You might come across a question such as $g_{2,1}$. Look for the number in the second row and the first column, which is 5; $g_{3,3}$ would be 7; and $g_{1,3}$ is 6. The first row is always the first one, and the first column is always the one to the left.

You may also come across cases where you are asked to add the numbers in a matrix. When you add a number to a matrix, all of the numbers increase by the same amount. The same can be said when you multiply or subtract things within the same matrix. For example:

$$3 + \begin{bmatrix} 4 & 5 & 6 \\ 5 & 6 & 4 \\ 3 & 2 & 7 \end{bmatrix} = \begin{bmatrix} 7 & 8 & 9 \\ 8 & 9 & 7 \\ 6 & 4 & 10 \end{bmatrix}$$

There may also be times when you have to add or subtract one matrix from another. In this case, the numbers are treated separately from one another as follows:

$$
\begin{bmatrix} 4 & 5 & 6 \\ 5 & 6 & 4 \\ 3 & 2 & 7 \end{bmatrix}
+
\begin{bmatrix} 7 & 8 & 9 \\ 8 & 9 & 7 \\ 6 & 4 & 10 \end{bmatrix}
$$

The first row has the numbers 11, 13 and 15. The second row features the numbers 13, 15 and 11. The third row has the numbers 9, 6 and 17. The numbers should all be treated separately.

Word Problems

Word problems are often included in the AFOQT exam, requiring you to read key information to determine how to solve certain math problems. These tips should help you when you encounter such problems:

1. Consider the data that appears to be most relevant

You might encounter a question that has certain details based on time, amounts and the number of subjects involved. Focus only on the details necessary to solve the problem. Part of the test is assessing your ability to parse key information and eliminate the unnecessary.

2. Identify the keywords in the question

Keywords dictate specific things that should be done when calculating an answer, such as the different operations needed. Some keywords include:

Addition: increased by, more than, sum, plus, added to, greater than, together, combined

Subtraction: decreased by, less than, minus, less, fewer than, apart, left over, smaller than, save, the difference between

Multiplication: times, multiplied by, twice, triple, each, by a factor of, a product of

Division: per a total, out of, a ratio of, the average of, equal amounts of splits, percentage (when you divide by 100)

Equal: was, were, is, gives to, cost, sold for

3. Consider real-world situations

Many word problems are grounded in real life. The goal of the testing process is to determine how well you can use your mathematical reasoning skills in a real-world setting.

The question might be that you have 8 hours to spend on a task. Use this information as a variable for the equation. You might see that something takes 8 hours to complete, and that you need to see how often it can be done in 2 days. Divide 48 by 8 to find that you can do the task 6 times in 2 days. Reviewing the specific situation discussed in the word problem may be vital to helping you identify a possible real-world answer to the question.

Math Reasoning Questions

1. What is 25% converted as a fraction?
   a. 1/4
   b. 1/5
   c. 1/7
   d. 2/9
   e. 3/5

2. What is the sum of 4/15 + 2/5?
   a. 6/15
   b. 11/15
   c. 2/3
   d. 4/7
   e. 9/13

3. What is the answer when you divide 24 by 8/5?
   a. 3/5
   b. 3/8
   c. 10
   d. 15
   e. 20

4. Which of these statements is correct?
   a. 1/3 > 1/4
   b. 2/4 > 3/5
   c. 3 > 16/3
   d. 5 > 30/5
   e. All are correct

5. What is the answer to 4,500/6,500?
   a. 0.534
   b. 0.615
   c. 0.692
   d. 0.782
   e. 0.853

6. One pound of wheat would cost $2. What would three-quarters of a pound of wheat cost?
   a. $1.25
   b. $1.50
   c. $1.75
   d. $1.80
   e. $2

7. The temperature in Celsius in your target destination is 3. The formula for converting Celsius to Fahrenheit is Celsius x (9/5) + 32. What is the temperature in Fahrenheit at your target destination?
   a. 37.4
   b. 35
   c. 39.8
   d. 40
   e. 42

8. (9 x 5) + (51 − 14) =
   a. 74
   b. 78
   c. 82
   d. 86
   e. 90

9. What is 9 cubed?
   a. 81
   b. 27
   c. 729
   d. 3
   e. 1/9

10. You achieved 15 of the questions correct on a test. Your grade for the test is 75%. How many questions were graded?
   a. 12
   b. 18
   c. 20
   d. 24
   e. 30

11. You took a question that has 40 questions, and you had a grade of 95%. How many questions did you get correct?
    a. 32
    b. 34
    c. 36
    d. 38
    e. 39

12. A car manufacturer produces 12,300 vehicles of one type, 15,400 vehicle of another style, and another 4,600 vehicles of a different type. How many total cars does the company produce?
    a. 32,300
    b. 36,000
    c. 29,600
    d. 31,500
    e. 34,400

13. You are planning a party, and you need 5 mustard packets for every guest who is going to be at that party. You will have 40 guests. Assuming every guest is going to have one hot dog each, how many mustard packets should you buy?
    a. 160
    b. 175
    c. 190
    d. 200
    e. 220

14. A retail store is offering certain shirts at 60 percent off. One shirt originally costs $15. What would be the sale price?
    a. $5
    b. $6
    c. $7
    d. $8
    e. $9

15. Your checking account had $6,000 at the beginning of April. The number increased to $7,000 at the beginning of July. On average, how much money did your account increase every month?
    a. $250
    b. $333
    c. $500
    d. $600
    e. $800

16. 15/3 − 10/3 =
    a. 5/3
    b. 5
    c. 4/5
    d. 3/5
    e. 2

17. Which fraction is the closest to 25%?
    a. 3/9
    b. 4/16
    c. 5/22
    d. 6/18
    e. 7/20

18. Which of these numbers is a multiple of 8?
    a. 42
    b. 48
    c. 54
    d. 60
    e. 66

19. In the number 324,634.5674, which digit is in the tenth position?
    a. 2
    b. 5
    c. 7
    d. The second 3
    e. The second 6

20. Round the number 346,235,794 to the nearest hundred thousand:
    a. 346,200,000
    b. 346,000,000
    c. 346,236,000
    d. 346,240,000
    e. 346,235,800

21. Which of these is the largest number?
    a. 3^3
    b. 8^2
    c. 14 + 5
    d. 12 x 4
    e. 50 + 10

22. Which of these fractions is the largest value?
    a. 5/10
    b. 14/28
    c. 10/15
    d. 12/18
    e. 9/12

23. What is the square root of 48 to the nearest hundredth?
    a. 6.15
    b. 6.93
    c. 7.34
    d. 7.85
    e. 8

24. -15 - -15 =
    a. -30
    b. 30
    c. 0
    d. 15
    e. -15

25. 15 x -5 =
    a. 20
    b. 75
    c. -75
    d. 20
    e. 3

26. -20 / -4 =
   a. 5
   b. -5
   c. 16
   d. -16
   e. You cannot divide by a negative number

27. In the equation 3x = 12, solve for x.
   a. 3
   b. 4
   c. 5
   d. 6
   e. 7

28. In the equation (x - 6) + 5 = 15, solve for x.
   a. 12
   b. 14
   c. 16
   d. 18
   e. 10

29. Complete the pattern: 5, 15, 35, 45, 65, _____
   a. 55
   b. 65
   c. 75
   d. 85
   e. 95

30. What is the easiest number to use when simplifying the number 28/14?
   a. 2
   b. 14/7
   c. 56/28
   d. 1 14/14
   e. A and B

31. In the expression x ≥ 15, what could x be?
   a. 15
   b. 18
   c. 20
   d. B and C
   e. Any of these 3 would work

32. In the expression x + 6 < 20, what would be valid as x?
   a. 13
   b. 14
   c. 15
   d. 16
   e. 17

33. $(3^3 + 15) + (34 - 14) =$ _____
   a. 42
   b. 52
   c. 62
   d. 66
   e. 75

34. How deep can you factor the number 24?
   a. 2, 2, 3, 2
   b. 4, 6
   c. 2, 3
   d. 3, 4, 2
   e. 4, 4

35. When producing the answer to 45 x 35, which of the following is a partial product?
   a. 225
   b. 1350
   c. 135
   d. 335
   e. A and B

36. 10 + 4 (5 x 2) = _____
   a. 40
   b. 24
   c. 240
   d. 35
   e. 50

37. 0.45 X 0.1 = _____
   a. 0.45
   b. 4.5
   c. 0.045
   d. 0.0045
   e. 45

38. 34 ≥ ?
   a. 35
   b. 38
   c. 34
   d. 33
   e. C and D

39. In the problem x + 15 = 25, solve for x.
   a. 5
   b. 10
   c. 15
   d. 20
   e. 25

40. Which of the following qualifies as an irrational number?
   a. 9.5
   b. 2.345967
   c. -3
   d. 0
   e. 14/11

41. What is the answer when you multiply √4 by √4?
   a. 2
   b. 4
   c. 8
   d. ½
   e. -2

42. What can be interpreted as an integer?
   a. -2
   b. -3
   c. 1
   d. 5
   e. All of these

43. Express 2/3 as a percentage to the nearest tenth:
   a. 66.7%
   b. 67%
   c. 66.66%
   d. 66.67%
   e. 66%

44. 25% of 65 is: _____
    a. 18
    b. 14.75
    c. 16.25
    d. 20
    e. 25

45. Which is a correct statement?
    a. 4/6 < 1/3
    b. 1/3 < 2/3
    c. 5/10 > ½
    d. ¾ > 7/8
    e. 1 < ¾

46. 15 of the 50 households in a neighborhood have a microwave. What percentage of those households does not have a microwave?
    a. 30%
    b. 50%
    c. 60%
    d. 70%
    e. 80%

47. If you had 16 questions on the test correct and achieved a score of 80%, how many questions were on that test?
    a. 18
    b. 20
    c. 22
    d. 24
    e. 26

48. Your household spends about $80 on groceries every week. What is the closest answer for how much you would spend on groceries in a year?
    a. $3,840
    b. $4,160
    c. $4,000
    d. $5,200
    e. $4,500

49. Which digit is in the millions position in the number 945,134,678?
   a. 1
   b. 3
   c. The first 4
   d. 5
   e. 9

50. Which digit in this number is in the tenths position: 345.678
   a. 3
   b. 4
   c. 5
   d. 6
   e. 7

51. You are buying a new car for $18,000, but you must also add sales tax. The sales tax on the car is 6%. What would be the total purchase price after tax?
   a. $18,600
   b. $18,960
   c. $19,080
   d. $19,500
   e. $20,060

52. 26 + 25 − 21 = _____
   a. 22
   b. 30
   c. 50
   d. 74
   e. 75

53. A car is driving at 60 miles per hour for 2.5 hours. If the car was to keep on traveling at that speed, approximately how many hours would it take for the car to have traveled 500 miles?
   a. 6 hours
   b. 7.5 hours
   c. 8.3 hours
   d. 9.2 hours
   e. 10 hours

54. If a car can travel 120 miles per hour, how far could the car travel in 20 minutes?
    a. 30 miles
    b. 40 miles
    c. 50 miles
    d. 60 miles
    e. 70 miles

55. In the last 3 hours, you spend 30 minutes eating dinner, 30 minutes taking care of laundry, one hour studying for the test, and another hour watching television. What percentage of that time did you spend eating dinner?
    a. 16.6%
    b. 20%
    c. 25%
    d. 33.3%
    e. 42.6%

56. A family of 4 spent $80 to get tickets to a baseball game. Two of the people in the family are children who were eligible for a $10 ticket. How much did it have cost for each of the 2 people who did not qualify for a discount?
    a. $20
    b. $25
    c. $30
    d. $35
    e. $40

57. $2 + \begin{bmatrix} 3 & 5 \\ 5 & 6 \end{bmatrix}$ = _____
    a. $\begin{bmatrix} 1 & 3 \\ 3 & 4 \end{bmatrix}$
    b. $\begin{bmatrix} 6 & 7 \\ 5 & 4 \end{bmatrix}$
    c. $\begin{bmatrix} 2 & 4 \\ 5 & 9 \end{bmatrix}$
    d. $\begin{bmatrix} 2 & 6 \\ 5 & 6 \end{bmatrix}$
    e. $\begin{bmatrix} 5 & 7 \\ 7 & 8 \end{bmatrix}$

58. In the equation 25x = 75, solve for x?
   a. 2
   b. 3
   c. 4
   d. 5
   e. 6

59. A car company makes 16,000 SUVs, 12,000 trucks, 6,000 sedans, and 9,000 convertibles. Based on an estimate, what is the closest number of cars that are made by the company?
   a. 25,000
   b. 30,000
   c. 35,000
   d. 40,000
   e. 45,000

60. What number is in the tenth position in 3,342,567.923?
   a. 2
   b. The third 3
   c. 4
   d. 7
   e. 9

61. Round the number 684,450 to the nearest thousand:
   a. 680,000
   b. 684,000
   c. 684,400
   d. 684,500
   e. 685,000

62. Which of the following is incorrect?
   a. -1/5 < -3/4
   b. 1/5 < 3/6
   c. 2/5 > 1/6
   d. 3/5 > 2/7
   e. 2/4 ≥ 1/2

63. -1 / -1 = _____
    a. -1
    b. 1
    c. 0
    d. 2
    e. Cannot divide by negative numbers

64. If 45 x 0 = 0, then 45 / 0 = _____
    a. 45
    b. 1
    c. 0
    d. -45
    e. Cannot divide by zero

65. Which number would realistically appear on the right end of a number line when compared with the others?
    a. 34
    b. 57
    c. 31
    d. 40
    e. 12

66. What is 3/10 of 30?
    a. 3
    b. 6
    c. 9
    d. 12
    e. 15

67. 5 x (3^2 + 16) = _____
    a. 61
    b. 95
    c. 110
    d. 125
    e. 1,805

68. If you were to divide 15 by 4, what would the remainder be?
    a. 2
    b. 3
    c. 4
    d. 5
    e. 6

69. Which of the following is not a prime number?
    a. 13
    b. 33
    c. 43
    d. 53
    e. 73

70. Which of the following is a prime number?
    a. 19
    b. 39
    c. 49
    d. 69
    e. 99

71. Which number can be interpreted as an even number?
    a. 0
    b. 1
    c. 5
    d. 6
    e. 9

72. Which of the following is the largest number?
    a. 9
    b. 8^2
    c. 7^3
    d. 3^4
    e. 2^5

73. $0.12 - 0.012 =$ _____
    a. 0.11
    b. 0.1
    c. 0.108
    d. 0.112
    e. -0.112

74. Finish the number sequence: 20, 16, 12, 8, 12, 16, 20, 16, 12, _____
    a. 8
    b. 12
    c. 16
    d. 20
    e. 24

75. How would the number 45 be expressed to the nearest hundredth?
   a. 45
   b. 45.0
   c. 45.00
   d. 45.000
   e. 45.0000

76. (2 x 1000) + (3 x 100) + (5 x 10) = _____
   a. 2,350
   b. 5,310
   c. 1,350
   d. 2,350
   e. 5,130

77. What is the lowest number that you could produce when making a factor tree from 84?
   a. 2
   b. 3
   c. 4
   d. 6
   e. 7

78. What is not considered an integer?
   a. 120
   b. 5
   c. 0
   d. -34
   e. 6.5

79. -1^6 equals: _____
   a. 1
   b. -1
   c. -0.01
   d. 0.01
   e. 0

80. 3 / ½ equals: _____
    a. 1.5
    b. 3
    c. 6
    d. 4.5
    e. 2

81. What symbol would be used to state that something is greater than another thing?
    a. <
    b. >
    c. ≤
    d. ≥
    e. ≠

82. What can 30/35 be reduced to?
    a. 10/15
    b. 15/17
    c. 20/25
    d. 1/5
    e. 6/7

83. What should be solved first in a math equation?
    a. Subtraction
    b. Exponent
    c. Division
    d. Addition
    e. Multiplication

84. What is the closest whole number to the square root of 170?
    a. 11
    b. 12
    c. 13
    d. 14
    e. 15

85. What is the answer for ½ x ¼?
    a. 1/2
    b. 1/8
    c. 2/8
    d. 2/4
    e. 1/16

86. Two lines form an angle. The line that links the ends of those 2 lines is a:
   a. Third
   b. Segment
   c. Section
   d. Vector
   e. Addition

87. 0.2 x 0.02 is: _____
   a. 0.004
   b. 0.04
   c. 0.4
   d. 0.0004
   e. 0.22

The following number is to be used to answer Questions 88-92:

Review the number 3,467,912.58.

88. What is in the hundred thousand position?
   a. 1
   b. 2
   c. 3
   d. 4
   e. 5

89. What is in the thousandth position?
   a. 6
   b. 7
   c. 8
   d. 9
   e. 0

90. Which of these numbers has the least value?
   a. 1
   b. 2
   c. 3
   d. 4
   e. 5

91. What would be the most accurate rounding of that number?
    a. 3,500,000
    b. 3,467,900
    c. 3,000,000
    d. 3,467,910
    e. 3,470,000

92. How would you get this number to feature something in the 10 million position?
    a. Multiply by 2
    b. Multiply by 10
    c. Add a 0 to the left
    d. Add an extra decimal point
    e. Do nothing

93. Consider the numbers 35, 45, 55, 65, and 75 and remove the 75. The average of the remaining numbers is:
    a. Drop
    b. Increase
    c. Stay the same
    d. Indeterminable
    e. Not a factor

94. What is the middle number between 35, 45, 55, and 65?
    a. 45
    b. 50
    c. 55
    d. 60
    e. No clear answer

95. What is the range for the numbers 25, 45, 65, and 85?
    a. 45
    b. 50
    c. 60
    d. 65
    e. 75

The following is to be used to answer Questions 96-100:

Review the series of numbers: 15, 16, 18, 19, 21, 22, 24, 25

96. What number would have come before 15 in this pattern?
    a. 11
    b. 12
    c. 13
    d. 14
    e. 15

97. What would be the second number to appear after 25 on this pattern?
    a. 26
    b. 27
    c. 28
    d. 29
    e. 30

98. What number could be considered the median?
    a. 18
    b. 19
    c. 20
    d. 21
    e. 22

99. The range is:
    a. 10
    b. 11
    c. 12
    d. 13
    e. 14

100.   Is there a mode in this layout?
    a. Yes, it is 19
    b. Yes, it is 20
    c. Yes, it is 21
    d. No, there are no mode numbers
    e. The mode would appear well outside this range

Math Reasoning Answers

1. a. 25 percent would be one-quarter, thus resulting in the answer of ¼.

2. c. To solve, you have to expand 2/5 to 6/15 so that the denominators are the same. The 2 fractions can be added together to 10/15, which can be simplified down to 2/3.

3. d. You would multiply 24 by 5 to get 120, then divide by 8 to get the final answer of 15.

4. a. The number that the arrow is pointing at is supposed to be smaller than the other number in the equation. In this situation, 1/3 is clearly larger in size than 1/4, thus A is the correct answer.

5. c. You would have to look at the nearest possible solution. You could use 4/6 as a means of finding the closest possible answer to this question. This would be 0.666, although 0.692 is the closest, so C would be correct in this situation.

6. b. Take 0.75 and multiply that by 2 to get 1.50.

7. a. To answer this, multiply 3 by 1.8 (1.8 is the calculation for 9/5) and then add 32.

8. c. The 2 segments in parentheses should be answered first before you add the 2 together. You will arrive at 45 + 37 = 82 as the correct answer.

9. c. A number that is cubed is a number that is multiplied by itself 3 times. 9x9 equals 81, and 81x9 equals 729.

10. c. Divide 15 by 0.75 to arrive at 20. You could also figure that 75 percent of 20 would be 15.

11. d. You would multiply 40 by 0.95 = 38. This could also be seen as 38 is 95% of 40.

12. a. The 3 numbers should be added together.

13. d. You need 5 mustard packets for each guest and that you're expecting 40 guests, 5 x 40.

14. b. As 0.6 is 60%, multiply 15 by 0.6 = 9; 9 is the amount to be deducted from the non-sale price to determine the sale price; subtract 9 from 15 = 6.

15. b. There are 3 full months in which your account would have increased by $1,000. Divide $1000 by 3 =$333, the approximate amount that you would have received each of the 3 months. Remember to choose the closest answer.

16. a. Since the denominator is the same for the fractions, you only have to work with the numerators. Subtract the numerators from one another to get the correct answer.

17. b. 4/16 can be simplified to 1/4, which is 25%.

18. b. 48 is the only possible answer, as it can be divided by 8 to get 6.

19. b. The tenth position is the first number to the right of the decimal point.

20. a. The hundred thousands position is the sixth number to the left of the decimal point. Unless you are told otherwise, you would have to round that number to the nearest point regardless of whether you are rounding that number up or down from the original one.

21. b. Answer B is 8 squared, or 8 x 8, which would result in the answer 64.

22. e. A quick review of these fractions will reveal that they can be simplified to smaller or simplified fractions. These would be cut down respectively to ½, ½, 2/3, 2/3, and ¾. E is the largest, as it has a value of ¾.

23. b. The square root of 49, which is 7. You can use this to figure that the square root of 48 would be extremely close to 7.

24. c. Subtracting -15, which is essentially the same as adding 15, so the answer would be 0.

25. c. When you multiple a positive number by a negative one, a negative is produced.

26. a. When you divide a negative number by another negative number, a positive number is produced. The same can be said when multiplying 2 negative numbers.

27. b. Divide 12 by 3 = 4, the correct answer.

28. c. Subtract 5 from 15 = 10 and x =16; 16 − 6 = 10.

29. c. The pattern is alternating between numbers that are separated by 10 and ones separated by 20. The last number would require adding 10 and 75 would be the next number in the equation.

30. a. The best thing that you can do when simplifying a fraction is to get as close to the whole value as possible so 2 would be the best choice.

31. e. The line under the symbol means that x is greater than or equal to 15. Therefore, A, B, or C are all legitimate answers.

32. a. 20 - 6 = 14. X should be less than 14, and A is the only possible answer.

33. c. The 2 parts in parentheses are to be solved separately. The cubed segment would be solved first as 27. The result would be 42 + 20 = 62.

34. a. 24 would go down to 4 and 6 on a factor tree, but it will eventually move down to 2 and 2 and 3 and 3. You can tell that this is the correct answer in that the 4 numbers would multiply with one another to get 24.

35. e. By multiplying 45 by 5 and then 45 by 3 with a 0 at the end of that one, you would get the 2 partial products needed to complete the question.

36. e. You would have to work on the part in parentheses first and then multiply that part by 4. When there are no punctuation marks next to a word near the parentheses, that means you would have to multiply that segment to get the correct answer.

37. c. You are working with 2 decimal points at the beginning and then multiplying that number by a number with one decimal point to produce an answer that has 3 decimal points.

38. e. The position states that 34 is greater than or equal to something. 33 and 34 are both possible choices.

39. b. Subtract 25 − 15 = 10, the number that would equal x.

40. b. This number cannot be written as a fraction, so it is irrational.

41. b. You are multiplying the square root of 4 by another square root of 4. This is 2 x 2 = 4.

42. e. An integer is a number that is not a fraction. In other words, any whole number could be interpreted as an integer even if that number is negative.

43. a. 2/3 could be expressed as 0.66666. This would become 66.666%, which when expressed to the nearest tenth would be 66.7%.

44. c. The equation is 4x = 65. This comes as you are working with one-quarter of 65. Divide 65 by 4 = 16.25, which is x.

45. b. The correct answer is 1/3 is less than 2/3.

46. d. The word problem is asking how many people don't have a microwave. You know that 15 of the 50 households have one, so that means 35 of the 50 households don't have one. Divide 35 by 50 = 0.7, and multiply by 100 to arrive at70%.

47. b. You would have to divide 16 by 0.8 = 20.

48. b. 80 x 52 = 4,160.

49. d. The millions position is the seventh to the left of the decimal point. 9 is the hundred millions place, while the first 4 is the 10 millions place.

50. d. The tenths position is the first to the right of the decimal point. 5 is in the tens place, while 7 is in the hundredths place.

51. c. 6 percent of $18,000 = $1,080. Add that to the original value of the car.

52. b. Compute the addition part of the equation first and then go on to the subtraction segment.

53. c. The car has been traveling at 60 mph for a while. The 2.5-hour note is irrelevant because the car is still going at the same speed and will keep on

doing so. The car is averaging a mile a minute. Therefore, you would divide 500 by 60 = 8.33333 hours, which can be rounded to 8.3 hours.

54. b. 20 minutes would be one-third of an hour. Multiply 120 by 0.333 = 40.

55. a. 30 minutes divided by 180 minutes for the entire three-hour period = 0.166, which is rounded off to 16.6%.

56. c. $80 - $20 = $60, which is what it would have cost for the 2 adult tickets. Divide that total by 2 = $30, the ticket price for each adult.

57. e. The numbers in the matrix are increased by 2 each. E is the only possible answer.

58. b. Divide 75 by 25 = 3, which is x.

59. e. By adding all the numbers, you would get 43,000. 45,000 is the closest number.

60. e. 7 is in the tens position, and 9 is in the tenth position.

61. b. The first 4 is in the thousands place. The number is rounded to 684,000 to the nearest thousand.

62. a. -1/5 is -0.2, which is greater than -3/4 or -0.75.

63. b. You will get a positive answer when you divide any negative number by another negative number.

64. e. It would be impossible for you to divide any number by zero. Therefore, E is the right answer.

65. b. The largest numbers are always going to appear on the right end of a number line. 57 is the largest of the numbers listed in this example.

66. c. 30 x 0.3 = 9.

67. d. 3^2 is calculated first = 9; 9 + 16 = 25. After that, multiply the total by 5 to arrive at 125.

68. b. The answer would be 3 with a remainder of 3, as 15/4 would be 3 and 3/4.

69. b. 33 can be divided by 3 or 11 and is not a prime number.

70. a. 39, 69, and 99 can be divided by 3, while 49 can be divided by 7. 19 cannot be divided by any number other than itself and 1, so 19 is a prime number.

71. d. 6 is the only number that can be interpreted as an even number.

72. c. The numbers would be 9, 64, 343, 81, and 32.

73. c. You can expand 0.12 to 0.120 for simplifying the process of answering this question.

74. a. The sequence appears to be going up and down between 8 and 20 with each number being separated by 4. The trend is going downward at this point.

75. c. The hundredth position would be 2 decimal places to the right of the decimal point.

76. a. To answer this, review the specific questions items based on what is utilized.

77. a. Since 84 is a multiple of 2, that would be the lowest number you can produce on a factor tree.

78. e. An integer does not have a fractional component. 6.5 has a fractional component.

79. a. Since the exponent of the negative number is even, the final product would be positive.

80. c. Divide 3 by ½. The rule is to invert the fraction and multiply which is 3 x 2 = 6. There are 6 halves in 3.

81. b. The > symbol means that something is greater than, while < means that something is less than.

82. e. Divide both parts of the fraction by the same number, as 6/7 would produce.

83. b. The exponent is the second thing to solve after the parentheses.

84. c. The square root of 169 is 13, so the square root of 170 would be slightly more.

85. b. The numerator is the same for each fraction, but denominators are multiplied.

86. d. A vector will produce a link that shows how far the 2 lines may go.

87. a. The problem is produced by multiplying the 2 and 2 together and moving the decimal spot one more position as you multiplying tenths by hundredths.

88. d. The hundred thousands position appears directly before the millions position.

89. e. There is no thousandth position here, but we can assume it would be 0.

90. e. The 5 is in the tenth position, thus it has the smallest possible value.

91. d. This is the one instance of rounding that is done with a more precise number. In this case, it requires rounding the number to the nearest tens position.

92. b. When you multiply something by 10, you are essentially moving the decimal spot to the right by one position, thus creating the 10 millions position.

93. a. 75 is the highest number, so removing that would increase the average between the numbers.

94. b. 50 could be the middle number, as you are looking at the midway point within the entire range.

95. c. There is a 60-number difference between the numbers listed.

96. c. The pattern shows that 2 numbers are consecutive and then skips a number before continuing with 2 more consecutive numbers and so forth. 12 and 13 would be the numbers prior to this sequence.

97. c. 27 and 28 would be the next numbers in this pattern.

98. c. 20 could be the median because it comes in between the fourth and fifth numbers.

99. a. 25 − 15 is 10, which is the range of the numbers.

100. d. The mode is the number that appears the most often. Each number here appears once, so there is no mode.

Chapter 5 – Word Knowledge

This segment of the AFOQT exam focuses on assessing your knowledge of the English language.

You will be required to answer a question based on what a word means, choosing from one of five single-word definitions. For instance:

Generous

    a. Giving

    b. Greedy

    c. Poor

    d. Conservative

    e. Controlled

Giving would be the best choice in this example. A person who is generous is someone who is giving. That person is not greedy or conservative, nor is that person poor or controlled.

You might be given a sentence that has a blank space. You will need to choose the word that best fits the sentence. For example, "The team is very _____ in working to win." A word such as "cooperative" or "adamant" could be used in this case.

Analyzing Words

The way a word is used can give a hint as to its meaning. This means you have to look at both the denotation and connotation of a word. Denotation refers to the specific definition found in a dictionary. Connotation refers to how a word is used in a sentence.

Many of the words in the English language are derived from Greek and Latin. These can help you determine denotation and connotation.

    1. Prefix

A prefix is a syllable or syllables added to the beginning of a root word to form another word. For instance, anti- is a prefix that means the opposite, as in antiestablishment or antivenom. Neo- is a prefix that denotes new or recent, as in neo-science; inter- is used to show relationship between items, as in interplanetary.

2. Suffix

A suffix is a syllable or syllables added to the end of a root word. For example, -able is a suffix that can be added to root words such as comfort, relate and infuse. Some other suffixes are -ion, -ish and –ize.

3. Root Words

Root words are the basic word parts without a suffix or prefix. A root word appears in between a prefix and suffix. For example, the root word of uncomfortable is comfort; the root word of indescribable is describe; the root word of unprintable is print.

Tips For the Subtest

1. Always review all the answer choices

You should not stop reading the question all the way through even if you feel you know the answer. Many people often get questions in this part of the exam wrong when they make guesses based on what they feel is right at first glance. Before you select your final answer, be sure to compare the word you think is right with the other choices available.

2. Recognize how a word is used in a sentence

Think about how you would use a word that you have to substitute for a definition in a sentence. Does the sentence make sense with the substitution? If not, you need to look at the other options available and substitute each in accordingly until you have the correct answer. However, you will have to use this strategy quickly, given that your time is very limited on this section of the test.

3. Prior to the test, increase your personal word knowledge.

Look at prefixes, suffixes or root words and build your knowledge of word meanings.

Word Knowledge Questions

Choose the best meaning of the following words.

1. Abridged:
   a. Standardized
   b. Shortened
   c. Entire
   d. Quickened
   e. Organized

2. Belligerent
   a. Proud
   b. Hostile
   c. Accommodating
   d. Greedy
   e. Thoughtful

3. Apathy
   a. Indifference
   b. Concern
   c. Care
   d. Laziness
   e. Fatigue

4. Anarchy
   a. Order
   b. Flexibility
   c. Pending
   d. Functionality
   e. Chaos

5. Charlatan
   a. Self-centered
   b. Accommodating
   c. Charitable
   d. Ignorant
   e. Forgetful

6. Deterrent
   a. Warning
   b. Encouragement
   c. Positivity
   d. Neutrality
   e. Accessory

7. Disseminate
   a. Illustrate
   b. Eliminate
   c. Draw
   d. Align
   e. Spread

8. Delete
   a. Remove
   b. Include
   c. Excise
   d. Control
   e. Amend

9. Credible
   a. Sensible
   b. Believable
   c. Outlandish
   d. Questionable
   e. Sure

10. Collate
    a. Arrange
    b. Reverse
    c. Take apart
    d. Combine
    e. Field

11. Derision
    a. Senseless
    b. Praise
    c. Complementary
    d. Sensible
    e. Mockery

12. Extant
   a. Alive
   b. Dead
   c. Possible
   d. Impossible
   e. Useful

13. Fundamental
   a. Strong
   b. Unnecessary
   c. Essential
   d. Optional
   e. Advanced

14. Mandatory
   a. Required
   b. Optional
   c. Striking
   d. Accessory
   e. Rules

15. Negotiate
   a. Demand
   b. Surrender
   c. Bargain
   d. Allow
   e. Supply

16. Mobile
   a. Movable
   b. Set up
   c. Heavy
   d. Light
   e. Stationary

17. Indigent
   a. Rich
   b. Controlled
   c. Poor
   d. Planned
   e. Organized

18. Benediction
    a. Blessing
    b. Dedication
    c. Remarking
    d. Opening
    e. Closing

19. Bastion
    a. Assembly
    b. Accessory
    c. Setup
    d. Weapon
    e. Fortress

20. Boon
    a. Transfer
    b. Gift
    c. Fix
    d. Weapon
    e. Hunt

21. Clamor
    a. Surprise
    b. Uproar
    c. Anger
    d. Intriguing
    e. Volume

22. Crux
    a. Focus
    b. Religion
    c. Value
    d. End
    e. Challenge

23. Dissent
    a. Disagreement
    b. Consensus
    c. Interest
    d. Amazement
    e. Standard

24. Fervor
    a. Fever
    b. Anger
    c. Uproar
    d. Disillusionment
    e. Passion

25. Milieu
    a. Values
    b. Collaboration
    c. Surroundings
    d. Attitude
    e. Concepts

26. Pedagogue
    a. Strict
    b. Laid-back
    c. Simple
    d. Flexible
    e. Freeform

27. Pretext
    a. Rationale
    b. Fact
    c. Idea
    d. Considerations
    e. Introduction

28. Rapport
    a. Confrontation
    b. Confusion
    c. Interest
    d. Friendship
    e. Worry

29. Satire
    a. Criticism
    b. Fact
    c. Idea
    d. Plan
    e. Satellite

30. Tacit
    a. Implied
    b. Direct
    c. Facetious
    d. Considerate
    e. Confusing

31. Snare
    a. Tie
    b. Twist
    c. Trend
    d. Trap
    e. Torment

32. Taint
    a. Poison
    b. Enhance
    c. Break
    d. Appeal
    e. Trash

33. Sanction
    a. Approve
    b. Shun
    c. Question
    d. Rule
    e. Idea

34. Pundit
    a. Consultant
    b. Idealist
    c. Consideration
    d. Question
    e. Expert

35. Pittance
    a. Excessive
    b. Sensible
    c. Average
    d. Minimal
    e. Vibrancy

36. Panacea
   a. Cover-all
   b. Specific
   c. Vague
   d. All-or-none
   e. Standardized

37. Overture
   a. Signal
   b. Start
   c. Layout
   d. Repetition
   e. Height

38. Amity
   a. Friendship
   b. Pride
   c. Disagreement
   d. Greed
   e. Generous

39. Deluge
   a. Trickle
   b. Flood
   c. Haste
   d. Speed
   e. Generalization

40. Connoisseur
   a. Idealist
   b. Free-thinker
   c. Pointer
   d. Sensationalist
   e. Judge

41. Diction
   a. Gesture
   b. Rate
   c. Function
   d. Speech
   e. Written word

42. Depravity
    a. Corrupt
    b. Sane
    c. Useful
    d. Interesting
    e. Questionable

43. Debacle
    a. Victory
    b. Domination
    c. Slight
    d. Surprise
    e. Failure

44. Epoch
    a. Era
    b. Literature
    c. Distance
    d. Control
    e. Conceit

45. Verbose
    a. Vehicular
    b. Verbal
    c. Audible
    d. Hasty
    e. Quick

46. Vehement
    a. Lazy
    b. Surprised
    c. Demanding
    d. Challenge
    e. Urgent

47. Solemn
    a. Significant
    b. Serious
    c. Considerate
    d. Light-heated
    e. Quiet

48. Resolute
    a. Planned
    b. Resolution
    c. Thinking
    d. Determined
    e. Unready

49. Profuse
    a. Flowing
    b. Planned
    c. Ready
    d. Lacking
    e. Stopping

50. Novel
    a. Classy
    b. New
    c. Uneventful
    d. Investigative
    e. Complex

51. Lucid
    a. Evident
    b. Cloudy
    c. Clear
    d. Established
    e. Planned

52. Pedestrian
    a. Extraordinary
    b. Dull
    c. Eventful
    d. Regular
    e. Scarce

53. Innocuous
    a. Vital
    b. Dangerous
    c. Sizable
    d. Unimportant
    e. Critical

54. Pervasive
    a. Odd
    b. Rare
    c. Unpopular
    d. Frightening
    e. Present

55. Frivolous
    a. Light-hearted
    b. Serious
    c. Unnecessary
    d. Fundamental
    e. Crucial

56. Extraneous
    a. Vital
    b. Interesting
    c. Sizable
    d. Relevant
    e. Irrelevant

57. Disparate
    a. Pointed
    b. Similar
    c. Worried
    d. Issued
    e. Different

58. Anecdote
    a. Cure
    b. Story
    c. Plan
    d. Arrangement
    e. Setup

59. Bondage
    a. Connection
    b. Slavery
    c. Frustration
    d. Reduction
    e. Constriction

60. Brevity
   a. Brief
   b. Lengthy
   c. Planned
   d. Arranged
   e. Considerate

61. Caste
   a. Class
   b. Concept
   c. Idea
   d. Value
   e. Point

62. Chagrin
   a. Surprise
   b. Pleasure
   c. Thrill
   d. Anger
   e. Embarrassment

63. Conundrum
   a. Riddle
   b. Plan
   c. Story
   d. Confusion
   e. Fright

64. Epitome
   a. Zenith
   b. Apex
   c. Start
   d. End
   e. Intermediary

65. Furor
   a. Plan
   b. Control
   c. Outburst
   d. Change
   e. Consideration

66. Tantalize:
    a. Plead
    b. Elevate
    c. Eliminate
    d. Entice
    e. Torment

67. Compensate
    a. Reimburse
    b. Tax
    c. Threaten
    d. Complain
    e. Remove

68. Skittish
    a. Uncomfortable
    b. Calm
    c. Sarcastic
    d. Confused
    e. Hyperactive

69. Tense
    a. Angry
    b. Happy
    c. Greedy
    d. Generous
    e. Uneasy

70. Capable
    a. Unable
    b. Trained
    c. Fearful
    d. Culpable
    e. Functional

71. Mitigate
    a. Determine
    b. Project
    c. Confirm
    d. Lessen
    e. Amplify

72. Laminate
    a. Overlay
    b. Textile
    c. Copy
    d. Smooth out
    e. Wear

73. Motivate
    a. Encourage
    b. Supply
    c. List
    d. Disdain
    e. Appeal

74. Hazardous
    a. Threatening
    b. Dangerous
    c. Safe
    d. Enticing
    e. Concerning

75. Rebuke
    a. Reprimand
    b. Encourage
    c. Remind
    d. Reinforce
    e. Cite

For questions 76 to 100, choose the word that best fits the blank:

76. The goal of the test is to _____ your knowledge in what you understand.
    a. Clear
    b. Gage
    c. Note
    d. Fulfill
    e. Eliminate

77. The movie theater plays shows for paying _____.
   a. Objects
   b. Screens
   c. Studios
   d. Entities
   e. Audiences

78. The task involves a _____ cleaning of every part of the engine.
   a. Grasping
   b. Threatened
   c. Soft
   d. Calm
   e. Thorough

79. The general goal of reading the book is to comprehend each _____ you come across.
   a. Page
   b. Note
   c. Content
   d. Fact
   e. Concept

80. The sloth is very _____ and inactive.
   a. Efficient
   b. Slow
   c. Dull
   d. Crazed
   e. Prominent

81. The kitchen oven needs to be cleaned so it can _____ foods well.
   a. Dry
   b. Dampen
   c. Aerate
   d. Heat
   e. Freeze

82. The vacuum cleaner is helpful for when you need to remove _____.
   a. Crumbs
   b. Water
   c. Oil
   d. Leaves
   e. Dust

83. The fortress is very _____.
    a. Elaborate
    b. Calm
    c. Quiet
    d. Protective
    e. Plain

84. The kids built the tree house for _____.
    a. Play
    b. Storage
    c. Decoration
    d. Consistency
    e. Investment

85. The stockbroker rushes to get payments handled for _____.
    a. Loans
    b. Deals
    c. Concessions
    d. Values
    e. Trades

86. Hubris is a sign of _____.
    a. Generosity
    b. Happiness
    c. Consistency
    d. Pride
    e. Ignorance

87. Those who are not willing to spend money can be very _____.
    a. Concerned
    b. Conservative
    c. Convenient
    d. Condensed
    e. Converse

88. The shoe salesman is careful over how he offers products to his _____.
    a. Investors
    b. Patrons
    c. Family
    d. Strangers
    e. Participants

89. The consternation of the people involved showed a sense of _____.
    a. Panic
    b. Confirmation
    c. Focus
    d. Betrayal
    e. Anxiety

90. A baseball game will require 9 _____ in most cases.
    a. Frames
    b. Innings
    c. Quarters
    d. Periods
    e. Steps

91. The number of _____ on a vehicle's transmission can dictate how fast it moves.
    a. Gears
    b. Pistons
    c. Brakes
    d. Wheels
    e. Steering bearings

92. When you go southwest, you are going in the opposite direction of:
    a. Northwest
    b. Northeast
    c. Southeast
    d. South
    e. North

93. You would have to clean the mirror with the proper solution in a spray _____.
    a. Jar
    b. Bottle
    c. Can
    d. Bucket
    e. Container

94. Those who do not think about the past will not be _____.
    a. Prepared
    b. Forgetful
    c. Confused
    d. Understanding
    e. Demanding

95. The rainstorm produced a _____ surface around the garden bed.
    a. Refreshed
    b. Thorough
    c. Crowded
    d. Damp
    e. Tight

96. The rain produced a massive _____ that was hard to predict.
    a. Spell
    b. Layout
    c. Quench
    d. Dowsing
    e. Deluge

97. The sandy beaches can create a mess, especially when there are _____ sticks all around.
    a. Wet
    b. Slippery
    c. Firm
    d. Broken
    e. Annoying

98. There are many thoughts surrounding different plans for work, although the schedule should be reviewed based on _____.
    a. Planning
    b. Time
    c. Date
    d. Ideas
    e. Availability

99. The worker was very _____ about getting a task done on time.
    a. Persistent
    b. Worried
    c. Issued
    d. Anxious
    e. Calm

100. Anyone who is too hasty could be _____ for complicating the task.
    a. Chastised
    b. Noted
    c. Reported
    d. Factored
    e. Condensed

For questions 101 to 125, choose the closest meaning:

101. Vigilant:
    a. Watchful
    b. Forgetful
    c. Annoyed
    d. Surprised
    e. Planning

102. Symptom:
    a. Effort
    b. Cause
    c. Change
    d. Alert
    e. Sign

103. Sullen:
    a. Weal
    b. Silent
    c. Planned
    d. Cunning
    e. Ignorant

104. Tedious
   a. Exciting
   b. Thrill
   c. Challenged
   d. Curious
   e. Dull

105. Trivial
   a. Significant
   b. Interesting
   c. Trite
   d. Weary
   e. Curious

106. Rebuff
   a. Decline
   b. Accept
   c. Review
   d. Check
   e. Note

107. Notorious
   a. Unfamiliar
   b. Well known
   c. Surprised
   d. Not very popular
   e. Tricky

108. Impartial
   a. Biased
   b. Learning
   c. Fair
   d. Not aware
   e. Interested

109. Dilated
   a. Enlarged
   b. Shrinking
   c. Split
   d. Frozen
   e. Heated

110. Indolent
    a. Active
    b. Alert
    c. Not aware
    d. Lazy
    e. Distinguished

111. Conducive
    a. Ineffective
    b. Not caring
    c. Helpful
    d. Surprised
    e. Challenged

112. Deleterious
    a. Harmful
    b. Safe
    c. Attractive
    d. Appropriate
    e. Planned

113. Flexible
    a. Varied
    b. Open
    c. Rigid
    d. Inappropriate
    e. Challenging

114. Authentic
    a. Pure
    b. Unappealing
    c. Fake
    d. Planned
    e. Controlled

115. Assent
    a. Refusal
    b. Plan
    c. Acceptance
    d. Understanding
    e. Solution

116. Adamant
    a. Stringent
    b. Thoughtless
    c. Interested
    d. Free-thinking
    e. Open to ideas

117. Kerfuffle
    a. Concern
    b. Happiness
    c. Plan
    d. Ideal
    e. Thrill

118. Verbose
    a. Tense
    b. Brief
    c. Unclear
    d. Simple
    e. Wordy

119. Faulty
    a. Pure
    b. Error-laden
    c. Concerned
    d. Planned
    e. Routine

120. Septuple
    a. Five
    b. Six
    c. Seven
    d. Eight
    e. Nine

121. Mainstream
    a. Important
    b. Useful
    c. Common
    d. Inhibited
    e. Clever

122.   Crevice
      a. Hilltop
      b. Beach
      c. Gulf
      d. Opening
      e. Cave

123.   Desk
      a. Seat
      b. Table
      c. Couch
      d. Loveseat
      e. Recliner

124.   Counteract
      a. Control
      b. Accept
      c. Note
      d. Challenge
      e. List

125.   Fall
      a. Ascend
      b. Descend
      c. Turn
      d. Climb
      e. Run

Word Knowledge Answers

1. b. An abridged item is something that has been shortened.
2. b. A person who is belligerent is someone who is overly aggressive. The person may be hostile to others.
3. a. Apathy is a general feeling of indifference and disinterest.
4. e. Anarchy is a condition where chaos develops as there are no controls to manage society. The situation falls into chaos due to a lack of power or control.
5. a. A charlatan is someone who is pretending to be someone they are not.
6. a. A deterrent is something designed to warn people about the risks of some action they may be contemplating.
7. e. To disseminate something is to spread the concept. This may involve trying to spread a message to many people.
8. a. A deletion is the removal of something.
9. b. Anything that is credible is believable.
10. a. Collation is getting items arranged in some form.
11. e. Derision is an act of intense mockery as a response to something happening at a time.
12. a. An item that is extant is alive, which is the opposite of extinct or dead.
13. c. The fundamentals of something are the basic or essential.
14. a. Anything that is mandatory must be used or supplied and is considered essential.
15. c. The negotiation process is a form of bargaining and attempting to come to an agreement.
16. a. A mobile item is something that can be moved and is not stationary or permanent.
17. c. An indigent is a poor person who is without means.

18. a. The benediction at a ceremony is when someone gives the blessing.

19. e. A bastion is a stronghold or fortress that an army's forces may be occupying as a means of protection and to be ready for possible attacks.

20. b. A boon is a special gift to people as a token of appreciation, although sometimes it may be a part of a larger trade activity.

21. b. A clamor is a sudden uproar and may involve people being surprised or frustrated over certain actions or events.

22. a. The crux of a matter is the vital and basic point.

23. a. Dissent is when people who disagree over a situation or action.

24. e. A person with a strong sense of fervor is someone who has a great passion.

25. c. The milieu is a particular social surrounding that one is in at a certain time.

26. a. A pedagogue is a teacher who is very strict and may have some very specific rules.

27. a. A pretext is a reason or excuse to do something that is not right and can be based on half-truths in order to convince others that what they are doing or planning to do is appropriate.

28. d. Rapport is a condition that allows people to get along with each other and feel friendly toward one another.

29. a. A satire is an action or narrative that is critical of some action of others or condition in society.

30. a. Something that is tacit is understood or implied to others, but it is not something that has to be actually said.

31. d. To snare something is to trap it.

32. a. To taint an item is to poison it or to otherwise cause something to become harmful or dangerous.

33. a. A sanction is something that is approved.

34. e. A pundit is a person who is an expert on a particular topic.
35. d. A pittance is something that is minimal in size and often used in reference to money.
36. a. A panacea is considered to be a solution for all things or a cure-all.
37. b. The overture is the beginning of something. The term is used mainly in music as the beginning of a larger piece of work.
38. a. Amity is the concept of friendship.
39. b. A deluge is an enormous amount of rainfall all at once and which could result in a flood.
40. e. A connoisseur is a judge of something and referred to as an expert in one field.
41. d. Diction refers to a person's way of pronouncing words.
42. a. Depravity is corruption including engaging in hostile and dangerous actions that are illegal and are done with no real regard to others.
43. e. A debacle is a massive failure.
44. a. Epoch is a term that relates to time or a certain era that may last for an extended period, possibly for centuries.
45. b. Being verbose is being overly wordy and possibly too talkative.
46. e. A person who is vehement is someone who has extreme feelings and is passionate about a situation or thing.
47. b. A solemn event is something serious that may cause sorrow or fear.
48. d. A person who is resolute is determined.
49. a. Something that is profuse is seen as being free-flowing and often in excess.
50. b. Something that is novel can be seen as being new and different.
51. c. Lucid is being clear and sane.
52. d. Pedestrian as an adjective refers to something that is very common.

53. d. An innocuous item is something that is irrelevant or unimportant and does not threaten.

54. e. An item that is pervasive is something that might be present quite often and will occur quite often.

55. a. A frivolous thing is something that is nonessential and may be light-hearted in nature.

56. e. An item that is extraneous is something comes from the outside and is considered extra and not really of any importance.

57. e. When items are disparate, they are different from one another.

58. b. An anecdote is a story that can be light-hearted, unique, and interesting.

59. b. Bondage is the concept of slavery and involves significant restrictions in a person's freedom.

60. a. Brevity is being brief, short, and to the point.

61. a. A caste refers to a class of people. This may include people who are in one particular segment of the population.

62. e. A person who feels a sense of chagrin would feel embarrassed over something that took place.

63. a. A conundrum is a problem that may be complicated or hard to solve.

64. b. The epitome of something is the peak or the ideal example.

65. c. A furor is an outburst or act of frustration that causes an upheaval of emotion.

66. d. To tantalize is to entice someone or to put something wanted just out of reach.

67. a. To compensate is to reimburse or to repay someone for something spent or lost.

68. a. Skittish is to be anxious or uncomfortable.

69. e. A person who is tense is uncomfortable and stressed.

70. e. Capable means to be able to be fully functional.

71. d. Mitigation is reducing the intensity of something, or lessening it.

72. a. A laminate material is an overlay or layers that are fused together.

73. a. Motivation is the desire to take action and produce work.

74. b. Anything that is hazardous may be interpreted as being dangerous.

75. a. To rebuke is to reprimand or express disapproval.

76. b. Gage is a way of measuring something.

77. e. An audience is a group of people that gather to view, watch or hear something put on for their entertainment.

78. e. To be thorough is to analyze something completely and from all angles or to do something completely.

79. d. A person reads a book to discover facts.

80. b. A slot is often associated with being slower than other animals, thus making B the best answer to utilize here.

81. d. Heat is the best choice as it is what people often associate an oven with the most.

82. a. A vacuum cleaner may be associated more with picking up crumbs of items rather than trying to clean up other items that may be stuck in an area.

83. d. A fortress is associated with being a protective site that would take care of people in many ways.

84. a. A tree house is often used for children to play in.

85. e. A stockbroker is a person who deals in stocks and other investments.

86. d. Hubris is when a person feels proud of themselves and values the self more than anything else.

87. b. To conserve is to use something wisely or sparingly, such as money or food.

88. b. Patrons are also known as customers.

89.e. Consternation is being anxious and worried about a situation. It does not include panic or fear.

90.b. An inning is a measure a portion of a baseball game.

91. a. Gears are used in a transmission to influence the speed of a vehicle.

92.b. Northeast is the opposite of southwest.

93.b. A spray bottle is the most sensible of the answers.

94. a. Prepared is the best word to choose.

95. d. Rain can cause a garden bed to become damp.

96.e. A deluge is an immense amount of rain that can happen very quickly.

97. c. Something firm is generally hard and not soft.

98.e. Availability is the best choice.

99. a. Persistence is being adamant and willing to keep to a schedule.

100.   a. To chastise a person is to be critical and accuse someone of failing to perform.

101.   a. To be vigilant is to be aware and watchful.

102.   e. A symptom is a sign of something that is occurring.

103.   b. A person who is sullen appears to be quiet, but is also angry at the same time.

104.   e. When a person is being tedious, they are being very dull and not very interesting.

105.   c. A trivial item is something that is not very important and can be discounted.

106.   a. To rebuff is to decline something that is being offered by someone else.

107.   b. Something that is notorious is relatively well known, although it is not necessarily well known for the best reasons.

108.   c. Impartial means to be fair and non-judgmental.

109.   a. Dilation means something becoming enlarged.

110.   d. A person who is indolent is someone who is lazy and slow.

111.   c. When someone is being conducive, that person is being helpful and supportive.

112.   a. Deleterious is to be dangerous and potentially harmful.

113.   b. A flexible item is something that can work in many ways or has many uses.

114.   a. Authentic means to be genuine and true.

115.   c. Dissent is a refusal to agree, an assent is acceptance.

116.   a. Adamant is to be absolutely sure and refuses to be swayed or influenced.

117.   a. A kerfuffle is some kind of disturbance that creates a bit of panic and concern.

118.   e. To be verbose is to be wordy and long-winded.

119.   b. Something faulty is not perfect and does not work as designed.

120.   c. Septuple refers to 7, as in a multiple of 7.

121.   c. Mainstream is another way of saying something is common.

122.   d. A crevice is an opening, usually a split in a rock.

123.   b. A table is the only choice that is similar to a desk.

124.   a. To counteract is to do something that stops the action.

125.   b. A fall incorporates descending, as in fall off a cliff or to fall down.

Chapter 6 – Math Knowledge: Algebra

There are two particular sections in the math knowledge subtest that are especially critical. The first is algebra and the second involves geometry, which is covered in another chapter. Many other advanced aspects of math may also be highlighted in this part of the test.

Exponents

Exponents can be used in many situations that involve multiplying numbers by themselves. Exponents may be written as negative.

1. Multiple Numbers

Exponents may be used for simplifying equations where a number needs to be multiplied by itself many times over. For instance, you can use 12^6 to express that 12 is being multiplied by itself 6 times. The equation can be written as 12 x 12 x 12 x 12 x 12 x 12..

You also have the option to write an exponent with a ^. The ^ is easier to type than a superscript. Therefore, 12^6 may be written as 12^6. The meaning and answer remain the same. (Note: An even-number exponent produces a final answer that is positive.)

2. Negative Exponents

An example of a negative exponent is 2^{-4}. Start with the number 1 and divide it by the original whole number as many times as required by the exponent. In our example, it would be expressed as 1 / 2 / 2 / 2 / 2, or $1 \div 2 \div 2 \div 2 \div 2$, which would equal 0.0625. An easier way to find the answer is to multiply the whole number 2 by itself four times, which equals 16. Then invert the fraction (to make allowances for its negative exponent) and the answer is 1/16. Converted to a decimal (divide 1 by 16), this becomes 0.0625.

3. Exponent of 1

Any number raised to an exponent [sometimes also referred to as 'power'] of 1 equals itself. Therefore, 5^1 equals 5, for instance.

4. Exponent of 0

If the exponent of a number is 0, that means the answer is always 1. Therefore, 5^0 = 1.

5. Parentheses or brackets

Always solve whatever is in parentheses FIRST. There might be an exponent included in the parentheses. For example, (4×5^2) is $4 \times 25 = 100$. However, if you have $(4 \times 5)^2$, you need to first solve the equation within the parentheses: $4 \times 5 = 20$. Then perform the operation indicated by the exponent: $20 \times 20 = 400$. You could also write the equation as $(4^2 \times 5^2)$, and arrive at the same answer of $16 \times 25 = 400$.

Simplifying Algebraic Expressions

Simplification is used when algebraic equations include variables or unknowns expressed as x or y. Here's an example:

$5(2 + x) + 3(5x) = 140$

Start by solving the first part of the equation: $5(2 + x)$ Multiply each part in the parentheses by 5, producing the result: $10 + x$

The equation can now be written as:

$10 + 5x + 3(5x) = 140$

Next, multiply the 5x by 3, which equals 15x. The equation can now be written as:

$10 + 5x + 15x = 140$

Now add 5x and 15x together. This equals 20x and gives you a final simplified equation:

$10 + 20x = 140$

Move the 10 across the equal sign, making the 10 a negative number. Now the equation is:

$20x = 140 - 10$. $20x = 130$. Transfer the 20 across the equal sign in order to change it from multiplication to division. Now the equation is $x = 130 \div 20 = 6.5$. Therefore, x equals 6.

Relations

Relations in algebra involves a series of ordered pairs that include several numbers linked together to produce a series of totals. Here is an example of a series of ordered pairs written in a relations equation:

{(3, 5) (4, 7) (6, 8)}

In this, each pair of numbers in one set of parentheses is an ordered pair. The first of the two numbers (in this case, 3) is known as the domain. The second of those numbers is labeled the range (in this case, 5).

Relations indicate how numbers relate to one another. When you input a domain, you will get a range within the ordered pair. Think of this as being at a vending machine and ordering something that is a specific price. The domain is the item you purchase, and the range is the price.

Functions

A function in algebra states that there is one answer for x in an equation that depends on the value of y. For instance, you have an equation that has two variables, x and y, each with values. You may encounter a question where the value of one of the variables represents a certain total. A function states that if x is a certain number, then y is a different number.

Consider the following equation:

$y = x + 5$

A function would be that one of those two variables is worth a certain amount. You may see the equation with $f(x)$, but x is a specific number. For $f(3)$, the assumption is $x = 3$. At this point, you add 3 to 5 to equal 8. Therefore, $f(3)$ causes y to equal 8.

You can tell if a function is linear based on the following equation:

$f(x) = mx + b$

$f(x)$ is the value, m is the slope of a line, x is the x-coordinate and b is the value where $x = 0$ or the y-coordinate where the line will cross the y-axis on a plane.

You can use this to figure out the value of the equation based on the slope. If m is positive, that means the line is moving upward. If m is negative, the line moves down.

To get a better idea of this, we can look at the example of x = -1 and find the value of f(x) for f(x) = 3x + 5. In this case, multiply 3 by -1 to get -3, which you should then add 5 to produce an answer of 2. In other words, f(-1) = 2.

Equations and Inequalities

Equations and inequalities express relationships between numbers and denote whether the expressions are equal or not. Anything that can be considered equal is written as =, while anything that is not equal is written as ≠.

Consider the following problem:

For 4x + 8 = 34, could x = 7.5?

First, isolate x by transferring 8 across the equal sign so it becomes -8. The equation looks like this: 4x = 34 − 8, which is 4x = 26. Now transfer the 4, which is a multiplying factor, across the equal sign, and it becomes 'divided by 4'. Now the equation is: x = 26 ÷ 4 = 6.5. Therefore, the answer is not x = 7.5, but rather x ≠ 7.5.

You may also encounter equations that use the < and > symbols alongside ≤ and ≥. Let's go back to the equation used earlier and write it as: 4x + 8 > 34. You could be asked if x = 7.5 is a possible answer. To check if this is correct, find the value of 4x by multiplying 7.5 by 4, for a solution of 30. Now, add 8 to get 38, which confirms that 7.5 can be x in the equation as it is greater than 34 (also written as > 34).

Writing Equations for Word Problems

After reading a word problem, you have to extrapolate an equation in order to solve the problem. To do this, you have to analyze the meaning of the question and take note of the particular key terms that will directly influence calculations. Here is an example of how you can convert a word problem into an equation.

Sally regularly goes to the hair salon every month. She gets about 3 inches of hair cut off during each visit. If b is the length of her hair before she gets it cut and that length is 7 inches, a is the length of the hair after the cut, what would be the equation for this? We know that b = 7.

In this equation, b is the length of the hair before it is cut, and Sally always get 3 inches cut off during her visits. Your goal would be to find a, the total for the length of hair after it is cut. The equation starts as:

$a = b - 3$

But when we substitute b for 7, the equation is:

$a = 7 - 3$

$a = 4$

You will especially need to review the words used in the problem. Such words may include "added to," "less than," "removed from" and much more. The trick is to determine what the question asks for: time, money, inches, gallons, etc. That will always be the 'a' of your equation or the unknown quantity.

Graphing

Statistics is a part of algebra that involves finding relationships between numbers. You can use information in a graph to determine how different forms of data relate to one another.

1. Coordinate Plane

A coordinate plane, which features two axes, the x and y, can be used to help you identify how different data sets relate to one another on the same plane. The x-axis is the horizontal plane, while the y-axis is the vertical plane. The plane will help you organize data so you can compare it as needed to other information.

The points that you plot on a coordinate plane will be arranged based on which particular numbers they represent. Each point on the graph is designated by two parenthetically expressed numbers with the x number being first and the y being second. For instance, if you use a number that reads (3, 1), it means 3 is on the x-axis and 1 is on the y-axis.

2. Table

You can use a table to organize statistics based on the information you want to measure.

Many trends can occur in a chart. You may find statistics that compare things with one another and how those activities can change. For example, a chart may show totals that are in the thousands or the totals may represent other factors.

3. Bar Graph

In some cases, you might need to compare variables with one another. These include variables that are in the same field and which can be measured based on the same measuring standards. A bar graph may help you with this, depicting different items as compared to one another, sometimes using colored bars for clarity.

4. Stacked Bar Graph

A stacked bar graph is designed differently from a bar graph. You can work with individual bars on the chart, but the bars focus on comparing items that are similar to one another. This can help you with comparing data acquired from people in different demographics, for instance.

5. Line Graph

A line graph compares items based on the same measure and specifically works based on time. For instance, a line graph could show the annual changes in something over three years with each line representing a different year. This can be used to predict future values.

6. Pie Chart

A pie chart starts with a whole circle. Each slice of the 'pie' indicates a percentage of the whole. You can use a pie chart to compare statistical data and show the proportion of one piece of data as it relates to the whole.

7. Scatterplot

A scatterplot illustrates items that are measured based on two separate variables and is used to identify trends based on whatever data you are trying to measure.

You can also use the plot to determine what dramatic changes may be taking place at one time.

Collections of Numbers

On the test, you may come across numbers that relate to a measurement or a pattern that needs to be identified.

1. Mean

The mean refers to the average of a set of numbers. In order to find the mean, add up the numbers and then divide them by the total of numbers. Here is an example:

The given numbers are: 15, 17, 18, 20, 21

Add all five of these numbers together and your answer is 91. Next, divide 91 by 5 (the number of numbers in the given set) = 18.2. The mean is 18.2 and this can be rounded down to 18 if required.

2. Median

The median is the middle value of the numbers in a grouping. For an odd-number series of entries, choose the one in the middle. This includes the third entry when there are five number, the fifth entry when there are numbers and so forth. Look at the example above:

15, 17, 18, 20, 21

18 is the median as it is the third of five numbers.

You might have an even number of entries. In that case, add the two middle items together. After that, divide them in half to obtain the median. Here is an example:

34, 37, 38, 41, 44, 46, 50, 52

41 and 44 are the two middle numbers. Add these two to get 85, then divide that number by two (half) to get the median of 42.5.

3. Mode

The mode refers to the number that appears most often on a layout. The mode can be utilized on a visual representation of data to reveal where a curve or other statistical analysis point will be most prominent. Here's an example:

4, 6, 8, 8, 9, 11, 13, 14, 16, 16, 16, 17, 17, 19, 20

Notice that 8, 16 and 17 all appear multiple times. 8 and 17 both appear twice, and 16 shows up three times, thus making 16 the number that appears most often. Therefore, 16 is the mode.

4. Range

In some cases, you might be given a range of numbers. The range is the distance between the largest and smallest numbers. You can use this to identify the variance between readings.

Look at the earlier example:

4, 6, 8, 8, 9, 11, 13, 14, 16, 16, 16, 17, 17, 19, 20

The highest number is 20 and the lowest is 4. Subtract 4 from 20, and the final answer is 16. This means that there is a 16-point range between the entries in the readout.

Chapter 7 – Math Knowledge: Geometry

Geometry is the study of shapes and their physical properties.

Parallel and Perpendicular Lines

1. Parallel

Parallel lines are always the same distance apart.

2. Perpendicular

Perpendicular lines will always intersect with one another and produce a series of right angles at the point where they intersect. Note how four 90-degree right angles are established in the middle where the two lines intersect. To figure out the direction of the lines, review their slopes. The slopes of perpendicular lines are negative reciprocals; that is, one line has a positive slope while the other has a negative slope. The slope is always the same for each parallel line.

Regardless of whether a line is perpendicular or parallel, you can use an equation to determine the slope. Take one point on a line and then subtract its x and y values from another point to the right. For y_1 on the example listed below, notice that (-3, 2) and (1, -2) are values on that line. The following is the equation:

(-3 – 1) / (2 - -2)

The answer to this equation is -4 / 4. The slope is therefore -1.

Meanwhile, the blue line has (-1, -2) and (3, 2) as plotted points. Take the numbers on the second point and subtract them from the ones on the first point. Therefore, (3 - -1) / (2 - -2) equals 4 / 4, which is simplified to 1. In other words, the slope of the line that is perpendicular to the one with a slope of -1 is equal to 1. The right angles formed show that there's consistency. If the lines have different slope numbers that aren't negative reciprocals, then those lines are not perpendicular, and they instead form angles.

Angles

Angles are formed when two lines intersect one another. You can identify the angle by looking at the vertex, the place where the two lines meet. There are four types of angles.

1. Right – 90 degrees

2. Acute – less than 90 degrees

3. Obtuse – Between 90 and 180 degrees

4. Straight – 180 degrees

A circle is a 360-degree angle because the line of the circle is uninterrupted and completes one revolution.

Circles

A circle is a shape where the distance between the center and the line forming the circle is the same. Circles have three key features:

1. Diameter

The diameter (d) is the distance across the circle through the center point and is used to measure the distance around the entire circle (its circumference). The formula for diameter is $C = \pi d$.

2. Radius

The radius (r) is the distance from a circle's center to its circumference. Use the following equation to find the circumference: $C = 2 \pi r$.

3. Circumference

The circumference (C) is a measurement around the circle. $C = \pi d$ or $C = 2 \pi r$

A note about π: The symbol π, or pi, is a mathematical constant and has the value of 3.1415926535 … (to infinity), or 3.14 or 22/.

4. Arc

An arc is a portion of the circumference of a circle. This is a fraction of the entire circle and forms a pie-shaped slice. The length of the arc is represented by 'l' in an equation.

For example:

To calculate the l of a circle with a circumference of 18 inches and an arc with an 80-degree angle, first determine the percentage of the whole circle which is represented by the arc: 80 ÷ 360 x 100 = 22.2%.

Next, solve for the length l = 22.2% x 18 = 4 inches.

Ovals or Ellipse

An oval or ellipse is different from a traditional circle. Although an oval has one line that produces a closed shape, ovals are oblong in shape. The distance between the central part of the oval or ellipse and the end will be different depending on which part of the triangle you work with. The measurement of the circumference of an oval is:

C = 2 x π x √((a2 + b2) / 2))

In this, a is a measurement of the major axis, the distance between the center of the oval and the point furthest from the center. B is the minor axis, which is the distance between the center and its nearest point. Multiply each of the axes by 2 to determine the distance between those points. Then, divide that total by 2. Next, find the square root. These problems are fairly unlikely to appear on the exam given their level of difficulty to solve without a calculator. Nevertheless, you should be familiar with them.

Triangles

A triangle is a three-sided shape whose three angles total 180 degrees. There are many types of triangles.

1. Equilateral Triangle

An equilateral triangle's three sides are all the same length. Each angle is 66.6 degrees.

2. Isosceles Triangle

An isosceles triangle has two sides with the same length and a third side with a different length. The triangle has one right or 90-degree angle, while the other two angles are 45 degrees each. The two lines of the same length form a right angle where they meet. The other two angles in an isosceles triangle are 45 degrees each.

3. Scalene Triangle

A scalene triangle has three sides that are of different lengths. This triangle has three different angles, although they will all equal 180 degrees when added together.

4. Acute Angle Triangle

In an acute angle triangle, all three of the angles formed are acute. In many situations, two of the three angles are of the same size, although this is not always the case. For instance, a triangle may have angles that are 55, 55 and 70 degrees.

5. Obtuse-Angle Triangle

An obtuse-angle triangle has only one angle that is obtuse. For example, a triangle with angles that are 30, 30 and 120 degrees is an obtuse-angle triangle.

6. Right-Angle Triangle

A right-angle triangle has one right angle (90 degrees).

Pythagorean Theorem

The Pythagorean Theorem is used to determine the hypotenuse of a right triangle. The hypotenuse is the side of the triangle that is opposite the right angle. The formula is as follows:

$BC^2 = AB^2 + AC^2$

In this equation, AB and AC are the sides of the triangle that make the right angle. BC is the side opposite the right angle.

For example, AB is 6 inches long and AC is 9 inches long. The equation is therefore $BC^2 = 6^2 + 9^2$ or

$BC^2 = 36 + 81 = 117$ inches

In order to calculate BC, find the $\sqrt{117}$ (square root of 117) = 10.82 inches

In order to quickly eliminate a few possible multiple choice answers, remember that $10^2 = 100$ and $11^2 = 121$. So the correct answer must be more than 10 and less than 11.

Area of a Triangle

Use the following formula to find a triangle's area: $A = 1/2bh$ or $bh \div 2$

The b refers to the length of the base on the triangle while h is the height. For example, the area of a triangle with a base of 12 inches and a height of 8 inches is: $A = 1/2 (12 \times 8) = 48$ square inches.

For an obtuse triangle, the base is measured and the height is taken as the distance between the base and the peak of the triangle.

Rectangles, Squares, Rhombuses and Other Four-Sided Shapes

A square is a four-side shape that has four sides of equal length and four 90-degree right angles. A rectangle has four sides and four right angles, but two of the sides are longer. A rhombus, which is diamond-shaped, also has four sides the same length, with parallel opposite sides, but the angles that are opposite each other have the same degrees.

A trapezoid has four sides with two (the top and bottom) that are different lengths and parallel. The other two sides are not parallel.

To find the area of one of these shapes, use the following formulas as applicable:

Square: $A = S^2$

Rectangle: A = width times length

Rhombus: A= S²

Trapezoid: A = top length(a) plus lower length (b) divided by 2 and multiplied by height, or A = [(a+b) ÷2] x h

Three-Dimensional Shapes and Volume

Many of the shapes you'll encounter on the test are three-dimensional. These three-dimensional shapes are measured based on their volumes.

The formulas for calculating volume in three-dimensional shapes include the following:

1. Cube: a^3 (square, a = length of a side)

2. Rectangular prism: abc (the lengths of the depth, height and width)

3. Irregular prism: bh (base length times the height based on an imaginary triangle going from one corner of a base to the opposite corner of the other base)

4. Cylinder: $\pi r^2 h$ (pi times the square radius on the base times the height that you calculated based on the base corners)

5. Pyramid: 1/3bh (a third of the base of the pyramid times the height the pyramid stretches out to)

6. Cone: $1/3\pi r^2 h$ (a third of the square radius of the base times pi and then the height)

7. Sphere: $4/3\pi r^3$ (a review of the radius of the three-dimensional circular item)

8. Ellipsoid: $4/3\pi r_1 r_2 r_3$ (the r values refer to the distance between the center of the ellipsoid and the nearest and farthest ends of the shape)

Regardless of what shape you are working with, volume is always calculated in cubic units.

Math Knowledge Questions

1. 5^{-2} is:
   a. 2
   b. 5
   c. -5
   d. 0.2
   e. 0.02

2. 4^0 is:
   a. 4
   b. 1
   c. 0
   d. -4
   e. You cannot use 0 as an exponent

3. 6^1 is:
   a. 1
   b. 6
   c. 1/6
   d. -6
   e. 0

4. 4^7 is multiplying 4 how many times?
   a. 5
   b. 6
   c. 7
   d. 8
   e. 9

5. Simplify the equation $3x + 4(x - 5)$
   a. 7x − 20
   b. 12x − 20
   c. 7x − 5
   d. 2x
   e. 12x

6. What sign should be used in the blank: 35 + 34 _____ 58
   a. >
   b. <
   c. ≠
   d. A and C
   e. None of the above

7. A triangle has lines on a right angle that are 3 and 4 inches long. What is the length of the hypotenuse in inches?
   a. 4.5
   b. 5
   c. 5.5
   d. 6
   e. 6.5

8. A right triangle has sides that are 7 and 9 inches long. What is the approximate length of the hypotenuse in inches?
   a. 9.8
   b. 10.9
   c. 11.4
   d. 12.5
   e. 16

9. The largest angle on an equilateral triangle is how many degrees?
   a. 33.3
   b. 66.6
   c. 90
   d. 120
   e. 180

10. Which of these is an acute angle? (All answers are in degrees.)
   a. 65
   b. 90
   c. 125
   d. 180
   e. A and B

11. On triangle ABC and XYZ, AB is 5 inches and XY is 10 inches and BC is 4 inches. What would YZ be in inches?
    a. 4
    b. 6
    c. 8
    d. 10
    e. 12

12. One line is moving at a slope of 3. What is the slope of the line that is perpendicular to that first line?
    a. 3
    b. 0
    c. 1
    d. -3
    e. -1

13. A circle has a radius of 5 inches. What is its diameter?
    a. 1.75
    b. 5
    c. 10
    d. 15.7
    e. None of the above

14. A circle has a circumference of 14 inches. What is the length of an arc that has a 120 degrees angle?
    a. 4.333
    b. 4.666
    c. 5.333
    d. 5.666
    e. 6

15. What is the largest angle on an isosceles triangle?
    a. 30
    b. 45
    c. 66
    d. 90
    e. 120

16. The first 2 angles on a triangle are 46 and 38. The third angle would be how many degrees?
    a. 42
    b. 90
    c. 96
    d. 102
    e. 110

17. ABC is a triangle where AB is 5, BC is 11, and the hypotenuse of AC is 12. Is this triangle a right triangle?
    a. Yes
    b. No
    c. Depends on the length of the hypotenuse
    d. You would have to switch the hypotenuse
    e. This may not be a proper triangle

18. Charles scored 15 points during his last basketball game. He has been on a trend where he achieves one more point per game. What would be an appropriate equation to use based on the potential for him to score more?
    a. $15 + x = y$; x is the number of points he could score later
    b. $15 + x = y$; x is the number of games he has played this season
    c. $15 + xy = z$; x is the points he can get, y is the games since then, and z is the total point total he would get all along
    d. $15 + 1(x) = y$; x is the games since he scored 15 points
    e. Any of these may work

19. If 1 inch is equal to 2.54 cm, then how many centimeters are in one foot?
    a. 7.62
    b. 25.4
    c. 28.32
    d. 30.48*
    e. 54.43

20. If a line has a slope of 4, what is the slope of a line that is parallel to it?
    a. 4
    b. -4
    c. 1
    d. 0
    e. -1

21. If you have $4 and it costs $30 to buy a case of soda, how many cases could you afford to buy?
    a. 5
    b. 6
    c. 7
    d. 8
    e. 9

22. In the equation $2x + 10 = 14x - 5$, x would equal:
    a. 1.25
    b. -1.25
    c. 3
    d. Any real number
    e. None of the above

23. In the equation $10 - 5x + 2 = 7x + 12 - 12x$, what would x be?
    a. 12
    b. 1
    c. 0
    d. Any real number
    e. None of the above

24. There are 2 consecutive integers that are arranged so that $3x + (y - 2) = 411$. What are the values of x and y?
    a. 100 and 101
    b. 101 and 102
    c. 102 and 103
    d. 103 and 104
    e. 104 and 105

25. Two workers are working less than 21 hours over the course of a weekend. If the first worker is working twice as many hours in a 21-hour period as the second worker, then how many hours is that second person working?
    a. Fewer than 7 hours
    b. As many as 7 hours
    c. More than 7 hours
    d. Fewer than 8 hours
    e. More than 8 hours

26. You have a set with the numbers {25, 34, 54, 67, 68}. What would happen if you were to remove 25 from the set?
   a. The mean would increase
   b. The median would decrease
   c. The median would remain the same
   d. The mode would decrease
   e. The mode would increase

27. A review finds that people in a hotel are likely to have cereal from the complimentary breakfast. What would be a sensible probability of someone being likely to get cereal based on this point?
   a. 0.90
   b. 0.05
   c. 0
   d. 1.5
   e. 2

28. A line is moving through the point (1, 4). Which of the following is accurate?
   a. x = 4
   b. y = 4
   c. x = y
   d. y = 1
   e. A and D

The following is for Questions 29-33:

Using this range of numbers: {25, 18, 23, 28, 23, 33, 20}

29. What is the closest number to the mean?
   a. 22
   b. 23
   c. 24
   d. 25
   e. 26

30. What would the median be in this set?
   a. 20
   b. 23
   c. 25
   d. 27
   e. 28

31. The mode of this set is:
    a. 20
    b. 23
    c. 28
    d. 33
    e. There is no mode listed

32. What would happen if the number 33 was removed?
    a. The median would rise
    b. The mean would rise
    c. The mean would drop
    d. The mode would change
    e. None of the above

33. What is the range of this listing?
    a. 5
    b. 15
    c. 18
    d. 23
    e. 30

34. What can be interpreted as a statistical question?
    a. What was your last test score?
    b. What were the grades of the people in the class during the last exam?
    c. How did you hear about the text?
    d. What was your time in completing the test?
    e. What did you use when preparing for the test?

35. North Carolina has 15 electoral votes in the Electoral College. If there were 530 votes in the Electoral College, then what would be North Carolina's impact on an election in percentage points?
    a. 1.5
    b. 2
    c. 2.8
    d. 5
    e. 97.1

36. Oklahoma has 7 votes in the Electoral College. Kansas has 6 votes in the same Electoral College. What is the greatest impact in percentage points between these states based on there being 530 votes in the entire Electoral College?
    a. 1.1
    b. 1.3
    c. 2.5
    d. 4.5
    e. 5.4

37. What is the area of a rectangle with sides of 5 inches and 12 inches?
    a. 48 inches²
    b. 60 inches²
    c. 72 inches²
    d. 85 inches²
    e. 100 inches²

38. What is the area of a triangle with a base of 12 inches and a height of 6 inches?
    a. 24 inches
    b. 30 inches
    c. 36 inches
    d. 42 inches
    e. 48 inches

39. A trapezoid has a top base of 2 feet and a bottom base of 40 inches. The height is 12 inches. What is the area?
    a. 320 inches²
    b. 348 inches²
    c. 384 inches²
    d. 410 inches²
    e. 430 inches²

40. Each side of a cube is 4 inches long. What is the volume of that cube in inches?
    a. 16³
    b. 32³
    c. 48³
    d. 64³
    e. 80³

41. If the radius of a cylinder was 3 inches and its height was 6 inches, what would be the closest possible volume of that cylinder?
    a. 54 inches^3
    b. 56.52 inches^3
    c. 169.56 inches^3
    d. 678.24 inches^3
    e. 824.56 inches^3

42. A rhombus with a 45-degree angle would also have an angle of this vertex in degrees:
    a. 55
    b. 125
    c. 135
    d. 145
    e. 185

43. A rectangular cube has a series if sides that are 3, 4, and 12 centimeters in size. The volume for this would be:
    a. 36 cm^2
    b. 144 cm^3
    c. 36 cm^3
    d. 144 cm^2
    e. 72 cm^3

44. The surface area is expressed in what units?
    a. Cubic
    b. Single
    c. Square
    d. Quadric
    e. Volumetric

45. The volume is expressed in what units?
    a. Single
    b. Square
    c. Cubic
    d. Volumetric
    e. Quadric

46. What cannot be used to produce a hexagon?
    a. Six triangles
    b. One rectangle and 4 triangles
    c. Two trapezoids
    d. Two rectangles
    e. One rectangle and 2 triangles

47. A kite is like a rhombus but with:
    a. Different side lengths
    b. Unique angles
    c. Changes in volume
    d. A greater height
    e. All of the above

48. What is the next number in this sequence: 15, 30, 45, 60...?
    a. 65
    b. 75
    c. 85
    d. 95
    e. 100

49. For 3x + 3, which of the following would be incorrect?
    a. f(1) = 6
    b. f(2) = 9
    c. f(3) = 12
    d. f(5) = 18
    e. f(10) = 30

50. (3x − 5) + (6x + 14) can be simplified as:
    a. 9x + 9
    b. 9x + 19
    c. 3x + 9
    d. 3x + 19
    e. 18x + 9

51. 7(5x + 5) can be written as:
    a. 12x +5
    b. 12x + 12
    c. 1.6x + 1.6
    d. 35x + 35
    e. 35x + 5

52. If x = 2, solve 5x + 6.
    a. 13
    b. 14
    c. 15
    d. 16
    e. 17

For Questions 53-57, use: $4x + 3y - 6$

53. How many terms are in the equation?
    a. 1
    b. 2
    c. 3
    d. 4
    e. 5

54. Which of the following is a term?
    a. 3y
    b. 6
    c. 4x
    d. All 3
    e. None of these are defined as terms

55. What is not a factor in the equation?
    a. y
    b. x
    c. -6
    d. 3
    e. 4

56. What is a coefficient in the equation?
    a. 3
    b. -6
    c. x
    d. y
    e. All of the above

57. What is the constant in the equation?
    a. 3
    b. 4
    c. -6
    d. x
    e. y

58. What would $5x - 5$ not equal?
    a. $(2x - 5) + 3x$
    b. $5x + (-5 \times 1)$
    c. $5x + (-5 / -1)$
    d. $5(x-1)$
    e. $(5x - 3) - 2$

59. If $2x + 2 \leq 0$, then what could x be?
    a. 0
    b. 1
    c. -1
    d. -2
    e. C or D

60. What would be a linear inequality?
    a. $x + y = z$
    b. $X - y = z$
    c. $x + y \neq z$
    d. $x + y > z$
    e. Any of these may work

61. What is the answer to $c(7) = 7x$?
    a. 14
    b. 21
    c. 38
    d. 49
    e. 56

62. If 1 is to 4 and 2 is to 8, 3 is to:
    a. 10
    b. 9
    c. 12
    d. 14
    e. 15

63. A factor is an item in an equation that is multiplied by:
    a. Anything
    b. A negative number
    c. A positive number
    d. A root
    e. A square

64. If 6 = 2x + 2, what would x be?
    a. 1
    b. 2
    c. 3
    d. 4
    e. 5

65. What word would work best when reviewing a problem relating to addition?
    a. Quotient
    b. Product
    c. Times
    d. Part of
    e. Combined

66. What word is best for subtraction purposes?
    a. Total
    b. Less than
    c. Product
    d. Shared
    e. Equal parts

67. What word is appropriate for multiplication use?
    a. Twice
    b. Increase
    c. More Than
    d. Combined
    e. Plus

68. What word can be used in a division problem?
    a. Reduce
    b. Fewer
    c. Remain
    d. Decrease
    e. Split

69. $2x^2 + 6x$ can be divided by 2 to equal:
    a. $x^2 + 3x$
    b. $x^2 + 6x$
    c. $8x$
    d. $10x$
    e. $2x + 6$

70. In $(a + b) (c + d)$, what should be handled first?
    a. Multiply a and c
    b. Multiply b and d
    c. Divide b and c
    d. Divide b and d
    e. None of the above

The following is for Questions 71-75:

There are 4 coordinates on a chart:

$a = (-3, 7)$
$b = (4, 7)$
$c = (-3, -5)$
$d = (4, -5)$

71. Which of the following is at the lowest part of the chart?
    a. A
    b. B
    c. C
    d. D
    e. C and D

72. How many points are between A and C?
    a. 2
    b. 6
    c. 10
    d. 11
    e. 12

73. The lines formed between A and B and between C and D are:
    a. Parallel
    b. Intersecting
    c. Perpendicular to one another
    d. Random
    e. Descending downward

74. What can be said about the lines between A and C and between B and D?
    a. They are horizontal
    b. They are the same length
    c. They are each slanted from left to right
    d. They create a single right angle as they intersect
    e. They produce unique angles

75. Based on the coordinates listed, what shape would be formed by the 4 points?
    a. Trapezoid
    b. Parallelogram
    c. Cylinder
    d. Rectangle
    e. Square

76. It costs $5 to buy one item and $25 to buy 5 items. What would it cost to buy 20 items?
    a. $50
    b. $100
    c. $150
    d. $200
    e. $250

77. What type of graph is useful when summarizing how a quantity changes over time?
    a. Pie chart
    b. Line chart
    c. Stacked bar graph
    d. Bar graph
    e. Histogram

78. A pie chart is designed to show:
    a. How variables compare
    b. Changes in values in time
    c. How much items are worth

d. Adjustments based on variables

e. Percentages of a whole

79. To compare 2 variables with one another, you should use a:
   a. Pie chart
   b. Bar chart
   c. Line graph
   d. Stacked bar chart
   e. Histograph

80. A stacked bar graph is used to compare:
   a. Historic changes
   b. Geographic positions
   c. Changes in actions
   d. Time-based movements
   e. Many variables

81. A scatterplot will include many points showing:
   a. Individual items in a study
   b. Singular variables
   c. Historical changes
   d. Proportions of items
   e. All of the above

82. A Venn diagram would show:
   a. Items that are different based on qualities
   b. Items that share certain qualities
   c. The historical changes
   d. A and B
   e. A, B, and C

83. Central tendency entails items on a chart being:
   a. Spread out evenly
   b. Skewed in one direction or point
   c. Mixed in many forms
   d. Items repeating many times over
   e. None of the above

84. The x-axis on a chart is drawn:
    a. Left to right
    b. Up and down
    c. Diagonally
    d. In any order depending on what the instructions on a chart state
    e. Circular

85. Which of the following questions is statistical?
    a. Do you enjoy turkey?
    b. What is your age?
    c. How well do you run?
    d. What is your history with driving?
    e. What is the average age of people in your neighborhood?

86. When a bell graph is at a normal distribution, it means:
    a. The mode is high
    b. The median is high
    c. The mean is high
    d. The mode, median, and mean are the same
    e. The statistics all around are diverse

87. What is the median of the number set of 4, 5, 6, and 7?
    a. 4.5
    b. 5
    c. 5.5
    d. 6
    e. No median listed here

88. What should you use when calculating math problems using π?
    a. 3.14
    b. 22/7
    c. 3.1
    d. 3.2
    e. A or B

89. What type of angle would be a straight line based on degrees?
    a. 90
    b. 120
    c. 150
    d. 170
    e. 180

90. Which of the following is an obtuse-angle based on degrees?
    a. 90.3
    b. 90
    c. 88.5
    d. 85.3
    e. 180

91. What represents a 2-dimentional shape?
    a. Cylinder
    b. Sphere
    c. Cube
    d. Cone
    e. Trapezoid

92. Which of the following represents a 3-dimentional figure?
    a. Cube
    b. Sphere
    c. Cone
    d. A and B
    e. A, B, and C

93. If the sides of a square are 10 inches, what is the perimeter?
    a. 20
    b. 30
    c. 40
    d. 100
    e. 200

94. If the base of a triangle is 5 inches and its height is 10 inches, what is the area in square inches?
    a. 15
    b. 25
    c. 50
    d. 100
    e. It is in inches, not square inches

95. The angles produced by the lines connecting the 2 bases of a trapezoid would be:
    a. Acute
    b. Right
    c. Obtuse
    d. Straight
    e. It depends on the shape of the trapezoid.

96. What part of a rectangular prism is the smallest in size?
    a. Front
    b. Top
    c. Side
    d. Back
    e. Inside

97. If one side of a triangle is 6 inches and the other is 4 inches, how long would the hypotenuse be in inches?
    a. 5
    b. 6.58
    c. 7.01
    d. 7.21
    e. 7.95

98. How many seconds equal one hour?
    a. 1,440
    b. 2,500
    c. 3,000
    d. 3,600
    e. 5,200

99. How many weeks are there in one year, based on a year with 365 days?
    a. 51.54
    b. 52
    c. 52.14
    d. 52.65
    e. 53

100.   If you have to spend $3 per gallon for gas, what would it cost for you to have a 12-gallon tank filled?
    a. $30
    b. $36
    c. $39
    d. $40
    e. $42

The following table is for Questions 101-107:

State Capitals by Population and Size

Capital	State	Population (in thousands)	Area (in square miles)
Albany	New York	97	21.4
Austin	Texas	790	251.5
Boston	Massachusetts	617	48.4
Columbus	Georgia	210	879
Helena	Montana	28	14
Lansing	Michigan	114	35
Raleigh	North Carolina	403	114.6
Salt Lake City	Utah	186	109.1
Topeka	Kansas	127	56
Trenton	New Jersey	84	7.66

101.   Which of the following capitals has the largest area?
    a. Austin
    b. Helena
    c. Topeka
    d. Raleigh

102.   Which of the following has a population of less than 100,000?
    a. Salt Lake City
    b. Trenton
    c. Boston
    d. Raleigh

103.   Which state is last in alphabetical order on this listing?
   a. Utah
   b. West Virginia
   c. Virginia
   d. Wyoming

104.   The area of Salt Lake City is about twice the area of what city on this chart?
   a. Topeka
   b. Helena
   c. Lansing
   d. Albany

105.   Which of the following capitals is paired with the wrong state?
   a. Albany
   b. Boston
   c. Helena
   d. Columbus

106.   Are the capitals listed in alphabetical order?
   a. All of them
   b. The first half
   c. The second half
   d. None of them

107.   How many total entries are on this list?
   a. 8
   b. 10
   c. 12
   d. 14

Math Knowledge Answers

1. d. You are dividing 5 by itself, thus producing 1/5 or 0.2.
2. b. The answer to any question where the exponent is 0 is always 1.
3. b. When you use an exponent of 1, the answer is always the number on its own. In this case, the answer is 6.
4. c. The exponent always refers to the number of times that you have to multiply a number by.
5. a. You would take 4(x − 5) to get 4x − 20. You can add 3x with 4x to get 7x − 20 at the end.
6. d. The ≠ symbol means that something is not equal to another thing.
7. b. The Pythagorean Theorem states that when considering a right-angled triangle, "a squared plus b squared = c squared' and c is the hypotenuse. Therefore, 3^2 + 4^2 would be 9 + 16, which equals 25. The square root of 25 is 5.
8. c. 49 + 81 = 130. The closest roots to 130 are 122 and 144 for the squares of 11 and 12, so C would be the most logical answer.
9. b. The 3 angles on an equilateral triangle are all the same size, which would be 66.6 degrees each.
10. a. An acute angle is less than 90 degrees, so A would be the only answer.
11. c. The triangle is shaped so that XYZ is twice the size of ABC, so YZ would be twice the length of BC.
12. d. The slope of a line that is perpendicular to another would be the opposite of the other line.
13. c. The radius is half the length of the diameter.
14. b. Take the circumference of 14 and multiply it by 120/360 to get 4.666, the length of the arc at 120 degrees.

15. d. The largest angle on an isosceles triangle is 90 degrees, while the other 2 angles are 45 degrees each.

16. c. Since the sum of the 3 angles in a triangle is always 180 degrees, you would have to subtract 46 and 38 from 180 to get the correct answer.

17. b. By using the Pythagorean Theorem, calculate 25 + 121 = 146. This is slightly above 144, which is 12 squared. Therefore, the triangle is not quite a right triangle, as the angle would be a little off from 90 degrees.

18. d. Since the total goes up by 1 with each game, use x as a variable based on the number of games that have been played since scoring 15 points that one time.

19. d. Calculate 2.54 x 12 to arrive at the correct answer.

20. a. Parallel lines are drawn in the same direction, so the slope would be the exact same for each of the lines.

21. c. This question requires the answer to be rounded. You would spend $28 for 7 cases of soda. Since you cannot buy a part of a case, you would have to get 7 while still having a few dollars left over from the order.

22. a. Add 5 to the left to get 15, and then subtract 2x from 14x to get 12. This would result in 12x = 15. Divide 15 by 12 = 1.25.

23. d. The 10 and 2 on the left side would cancel out the 12 on the right side and 7x − 12x on the right is the same as the -5x on the left. Therefore, any number could be used on each side, as you would get the same answer regardless.

24. d. 104 would be reduced by 2 to equal 102. Then 3 x 103 is 309. 309 and 102 are added to equal 411.

25. b. The question states that one worker is working "at least twice" as many hours as the other in a 21-hour period. Therefore, a person could work 14 hours and the other would work for 7 hours. That is twice the total and

would mean that the second worker could work as many as 7 hours in the time period. The first person could work more than 14 hours.

26. a. The mean is the average of the numbers in the set. As 25 is the clear outlier the removal of that number would cause the mean to drop dramatically.

27. a. When the number is closer to 1 without going over, that means the probability of something happening is greater. A suggests that a person would have a 90 percent chance to do something. In the example, 90 percent would be the most realistic answer.

28. The numbers are listed as (x, y) and x would be 1 and y is 4.

29. c. If you add the 7 numbers together, it equals170. Divide the number by 7 which is 24.28 and 24 is the closest possible number.

30. b. The median is the number that is in the middle of the set. The number 23 appears in the middle.

31. b. The mode is the number that appears the most often. The number 23 appears twice, and the other 5 numbers appear once.

32. c. By removing 33, the largest number in the set, the mean would decrease. The median would be the same, as 23 is the third and fourth largest number. The mode is still the same.

33. b. Calculate $33 - 18 = 15$, which is the range that the numbers have.

34. b. A statistical question would include stats. A would be more detail on one score and would not qualify as something that could be used to help find statistics.

35. c. Calculate $15 / 530 = 2.8$, the percentage of votes North Carolina gets.

36. b. Since Oklahoma has more votes than Kansas, the answer would be calculated by Oklahoma's total of 7 divided by the overall total of 530 to equal 1.3 percent. A is incorrect, as that gives Kansas' total.

37. b. The area of a rectangle is the length multiplied by the height.

38. c. The area of a triangle is the base and height multiplied and then divided by 2.

39. c. You would have to convert the top base from 2 feet to 24 inches to complete the problem. Add the bases and divide by 2, then multiply by the height.

40. d. The volume is the cubed root of the side.

41. c. Multiply pi by the squared radius and the height to get the volume.

42. c. A rhombus has 2 pairs of identical vertexes.

43. b. Volume is always measured in cubic units.

44. c. Since surface area is area, it is measured in square units.

45. c. With a three-dimensional shape, cubic units would be used.

46. d. Two triangles put together will not produce a six-sided shape of a hexagon.

47. e. A kite would have an off-center diamond-like appearance to it.

48. b. The numbers are increasing by 15 in this sequence.

49. e. If x = 10, then the answer would be 33 and not 30.

50. a. The individual parts within the 2 parentheses can be calculated to simplify the equation.

51. d. 7 would be multiplied by both numbers inside the parentheses.

52. d. When a problem says "evaluate," that means you have to assume that x will be what it says it is.

53. c. A term is one of the items or one of the numbers in the equation.

54. d. A term is every part of one of these items and not a portion.

55. c. -6 acts separately from the other 2 terms and is not influenced by more than one item, so it is not a factor.

56. a. 3 and 4 are the 2 coefficients, as they are the numbers that interact with the variables.

57. c. -6 will not change no matter what happens in the equation.

58. c. You would arrive at a positive answer when you multiply 2 negative numbers.

59. e. C would give you 0, while D = -2. Either of these would work.

60. d. A linear inequality would focus on numbers that are either less than, more than, or equal to. The equation focuses on dramatic differences involved.

61. d. This would entail using 7 as x, thus producing 7 x 7.

62. c. The analogies suggest that the first numbers are being multiplied by 4.

63. a. The factor in an equation can be anything that you might want it to be.

64. b. Multiply 2 x 2 to equal 4 and then add 2 to equal 6, the answer.

65. e. An addition problem is items being combined with one another.

66. b. Subtraction involves a reduction in value.

67. a. Multiplication can be multiplying things by 2, so twice would be a sensible word to use in a multiplication-related question.

68. e. Division is a word that denotes splitting.

69. e. The x parts can be reduced by one each as you divide this in half.

70. a. The a and c parts of the equation are to be solved first.

71. e. C and D both have a -5 on the y-axis.

72. e. A and C are 12 points apart based on the y-axis.

73. a. The lines would go in the same direction and at the same slope, so they would be parallel.

74. b. The 2 lines formed are the same length.

75. d. With the lines being straight and forming right angles, they will form a rectangle. Two sides are longer than the other 2 sides of the shape.

76. b. The total suggests that you would have to spend $5 for each item, so 5 x 20 = $100 for the total value.

77. d. A traditional bar graph may be used to show differences in certain things and how they might change over time.

78. e. The pie chart would represent a whole with each segment being a small percentage of the whole.

79. c. The line chart may illustrate changes between 2 variables, or maybe things that may change when 2 items are compared with one another.

80. e. Multiple variables can be listed on the same stacked bar chart. Each bar has several shaded features.

81. a. The scatterplot is used to plot many different items that you are identifying in a single study.

82. d. The Venn diagram shows 2 or more circles of items with different variables based on certain qualities, and certain items that appear in intersecting circles share particular qualities.

83. b. The central tendency is that items are listed at various spaces depending on what is

noted on a chart.

84. a. The x-axis is the horizontal axis on a chart.

85. e. The statistical question requires a certain amount of detail in the subject being noted.

86. d. The normal distribution of a bell graph means that a perfect bell graph has been formed.

87. c. If there is an even number of entries, the median is the midway point between the 2 entries that are in the middle.

88. e. The pi constant is equal to 3.14, and 22/7 is very close to it.

89. e. A straight angle will always be 180 degrees.

90. a. Anything more than 90 degrees would qualify as an obtuse-angle up to just before reaching180 degrees.

91. e. A shape is a two-dimensional item.

92. e. Anything that is three-dimensional in nature can be considered a solid.

93. c. The perimeter is the measurement around the figure or the sum of the lengths of each side. Since each of the sides of the square is 10 inches, that means the perimeter is 40 inches.

94. b. The area of a triangle is measured by half the product of the base and height.

95. b. Since the bases of the trapezoid would be parallel with one another, the angles produced when a line is added would be right.

96. c. The sides of the prism should be smaller, and the sides would essentially be the bases.

97. d. Following the Pythagorean Theorem: 36 + 16 = 52. The square root of 52 would be more than 7, so D would be the most sensible answer choice.

98. d. Multiple 60 seconds by 60 minutes to get the correct answer.

99. c. Although people typically associate a year is 52 weeks, the correct answer is 52.14.

100.   b. 12 and multiplied by 3 = 36.

101.   a. Austin has the largest visible area.

102.   b. There are only 3 cities that qualify.

103.   a. The entries were already in alphabetical order.

104.   a. The result is the closest total you can find in this review.

105.   d. Columbus is the capital of Ohio, not Georgia. Atlanta is the capital of Georgia.

106.   a. A quick review of the list shows that they are in the proper order.

107.   b. The answer can be gathered through a fast review of the chart.

Chapter 8 – Reading Comprehension

Reading comprehension is vital for any job in the Air Force. As such, this section of the exam will assess your skills in this crucial area.

The reading portion of the AFOQT exam will require you to read and analyze an extended passage. Some passages are narrative, while others are nonfiction. Each passage is followed by a series of multiple-choice questions.

Summarization

A summary is a shortened version. When summarizing something, always:

1. Review the major points that the writer is conveying.

You don't have to include every detail, just the main points of the passage.

2. Avoid including minor details.

Decide what is minor and what is significant.

3. Emphasize the main idea.

Note that paraphrasing is not summarizing. Paraphrasing requires you to read a passage and then rewrite it in your own words, not necessarily always as a summary.

Writing a Conclusion

A conclusion sums up the main idea of a passage.

In some cases, the end of the passage may provide new information that connects to whatever was at the beginning.

Three Key Points

There are three specific things you should take into account when reading. Always consider the:

1. Topic

The topic of the passage is what the passage is about. For example, if you are given a passage to read about the Washington Nationals baseball club, the topic is the Washington Nationals.

2. Main Idea

The main idea in a passage relates to a passage's core message. An example of a main idea is "The Washington Nationals have a fun game-day atmosphere." The main idea is that going to a Washington Nationals game is lots of fun. That message is then framed by supporting details to make the argument valid.

3. Supporting Details

The supporting details provide support for a passage's main idea/argument. In this example, the main idea that the Washington Nationals have a good game-day atmosphere might be supported by specific details such as how the ballpark has plenty of food options and affordable ticket prices.

Linear Content

A narrative structure is based on the linear or nonlinear content of the passage. A passage about a recipe may be linear because it goes from one instruction to the next. A passage that explains a list of things could be nonlinear as it does not have to fit a pattern.

A linear narrative is one that progresses in a certain direction. You are working with content in chronological order.

1. Exposition

The exposition is the start of a passage. It's the introduction of the topic and the main idea.

2. Rising Action

The rising action follows the exposition. It's the series of events that leads up to the conflict in a narrative.

3. Conflict

A conflict is the tension in a narrative. It can include character vs. character (such as a fight), character vs. self (a difficult decision one has to make), character vs. nature (an earthquake or a shark attack, for example), or character vs. society (someone fighting racism, for instance).

4. Climax

The climax is the culmination of the rising action and climax. At the climax, a major revelation or sudden development will occur. The climax is always the most exciting moment in a narrative (i.e., someone is rescued or a mystery is solved).

5. Falling Action

Since the climax is the apex of the story, there is nowhere to go but down from there. The falling action is a series of events that proceeds toward the end (resolution) of the story.

6. Resolution

The resolution marks the end of the story. The reader should be satisfied, and all loose threads in a narrative should be resolved.

Of course, you may come across different structures when you're working with linear points that go beyond a narrative. You may encounter a passage that includes several steps to solve a problem or accomplish a task. The exposition would be the outline of the problem to be resolved. The rising action in such cases will be the many steps involved, and the climax is the point where the task is completed. The falling action is what follows after a task is finished—i.e., you've built a shelf and put books on it. The resolution summarizes the benefits of completing the task.

Nonlinear Content

There may be cases where the content you are reading is nonlinear in nature. What this means is that there is no distinct frame of reference to work with. The most common situation is that the content involved is relayed out of chronological order. Since nonlinear narratives don't proceed systematically from one point to the next, they're not predictable, and thus make a narrative more interesting.

In the AFOQT exam, you might notice something like the main subject matter being revealed in the last paragraph. The preceding paragraphs may contain many details, but you might not be fully aware of the main idea.

Facts or Opinions

You may read passages in the AFOQT exam that are factual in nature. These provide information that is confirmed and supported, such as a research study on the danger of smoking.

In other cases, the passage may be a writer's opinion that you either agree or disagree with. Opinion pieces may use a lot of adjectives or adverbs, leaning toward emotional language (both positive and negative). While a factual piece on the dangers of tobacco might quote doctors and list statistics, an opinion piece is more likely to describe a loved one who developed lung cancer and suffered terribly.

Biases can be frustrating because it is more difficult for people to trust the words of an author when it's obvious he or she is only looking at one side of things.

A stereotype oversimplifies a person or idea using purportedly common characteristics (for example, "all people in a certain culture do x" is a stereotype). Stereotyping typically involves a personal bias and may involve a person thinking that all people within a certain segment of the population are the same.

Comparison and Contrast

A comparison and contrast passages will include the following parts:

1. Introduction

The introduction will introduce the subject matter and give some background for why it's being framed as a compare/contrast passage.

2. First Item

The first paragraph may include a description which explains the relevance of the article.

3. Second Item

The second item should discuss something separate from the first, but should remain relevant to the main topic. There should be consistency. (Note: More than two items may be incorporated into a compare and contrast passage. You should focus on the main points.)

4. Reviewing the Items

The review succinctly encapsulates the information presented so far.

5. Conclusion

The conclusion is the end of the passage. It summarizes the passage's ultimate message and recaps any important points.

Context

Context is background upon which a text is being written. For example, a historical text requires an understanding of context to analyze what may have been very different beliefs in a certain era. The context of a word can also affect its meaning. For instance, the word "flight" can denote a commercial airplane flying or a bird flying. "Flight" could also mean something like a series of drinks arranged on a single tray. You can't determine the correct meaning of a word unless you know what context it's being used in. So, for "flight," unless you place it contextually in a bar, based on the passage you just read, you may mistakenly think "bird" instead of "bottle."

Purpose

Every piece of writing has a purpose. This includes the general rationale for why an author is putting words on paper, whether to inform, emote, entertain, etc. Often, a passage's title will give you an immediate clue as to its purpose. However, a purpose is not necessarily always explicit. For example, when Upton Sinclair wrote *The Jungle*, he had an agenda in mind to change how the meat-packing industry operated. But that agenda doesn't become clear until you've read quite a few chapters of the book. Ultimately, Sinclair's purpose was industry reform, but he doesn't outright say "I want this to change," so you have to draw your own conclusions based on careful reading.

Perspective

Be aware of the perspective of the article you are reading. You will come across one of three perspectives:

1. First Person

A first-person narrative involves narration in an author's or character's own voice. You can immediately recognize first person by its use of pronouns such as I, my, me, our and we.

2. Second Person

A second-person narrative puts you in the middle of the story. Specifically, the person is talking to you. This type of narrative is often used in an instructional context. This includes a case where you are being told how to prepare a recipe or fix a machine. You can recognize second-person narratives by the consistent use of pronouns such as you, your and yours.

3. Third Person

A third-person narrative involves a narrator observing things and discussing them from a distance. Sometimes the narrator is omnipresent and can identify the many thoughts and emotions of the people involved.

Sometimes a writer might use alternative narrators or perspectives to tell a story. While this is not likely to appear in a short exam passage, it may be incorporated in a larger work to illustrate more perspectives. This includes giving the reader more ways to see an action from multiple characters' perspectives.

Reading Comprehension Questions

The following passage is to be used for Questions 1-7:

The convention center features various amenities that are suitable for hosting special events. The center features about 500,000 square feet of space for various activities. This includes an exhibit hall that is about 200,000 square feet of space. There is also a large ballroom that is 50,000 square feet in size for major meetings and events.

The large ballroom area can be divided, if necessary, into 3 separate ballrooms of nearly the same size. This feature is ideal for special events or major conferences that have multiple speakers or sessions.

There are 10 meeting rooms of various sizes within the venue. Each room includes a series of chairs for guests. Tables, presentation materials, and multimedia items are also included in the convention center to make it easier for people to prepare and present their presentations.

The main mezzanine connects to a local downtown hotel. The area is decorated with appealing works of art from many local artists. The design of the mezzanine makes it an appealing site for those looking to promote their wares and those who wish to see unique activities and events at the convention center.

The last place to note is the exhibit hall. The hall includes room for nearly 700 booths in its largest layout. The lighting features can be adjusted based on the needs of the occupants. The drive-in ramps on the outside of the building make it easier for vehicles to back up and load materials for display in the hall. There is also a small concession stand in the exhibit hall for guests and exhibitors to enjoy refreshments throughout the day of the event.

1. What is the passage about?
    a. A conference center
    b. A meeting room
    c. A mezzanine
    d. A city hall

2. What type of audience would benefit from this passage?
    a. City planners
    b. Business operators
    c. Food vendors
    d. Transport entities

3. What makes the large ballroom area distinct?
    a. It can be divided into 3 ballrooms
    b. The area features adaptive lighting
    c. The room includes soft carpets
    d. The design includes many chairs that are preset in various positions

4. The exhibit hall takes up how much space?
    a. Half the convention center
    b. About 40 percent of the center
    c. About 30 percent of the center
    d. A little over half the center

5. Which part of the convention center links to a downtown hotel
    a. Exhibit hall
    b. Mezzanine
    c. Business conference rooms
    d. Ballroom

6. What decoration would you notice in the mezzanine area? This refers to something that was specifically described in the passage.
    a. Granite floors
    b. Marble tile walls
    c. Mood lighting
    d. Local artwork

7. How many vendors could be housed by the exhibit hall?
    a. 200
    b. 400
    c. 600
    d. Any of those numbers would work

The follow passage is to be used for Questions 8-14:

The Washington DC Metro rail system is easy to use if you understand the layout. The system uses 6 separate lines. Each line goes to different places, although some lines share particular stops. For instance, the Fort Totten station is served by the Red, Green, and Yellow lines.

You can move from one line to another by getting off a train and then waiting for the next train that serves the line of your choosing. This is provided you get off at a stop that is served by multiple lines. In some cases, you can stay on the same platforms, but in other cases you would have to move to a different platform within the same station. Check the posted instructions and explanations.

The Washington-Ronald Reagan airport is the only airport in the area that is directly served by the Metro system. The airport is served by the Yellow and Blue lines. You can take a Route 5A bus from the Rosslyn or L'Enfant Plaza station to reach the Washington-Dulles airport or a Route B30 bus from the Greenbelt station to reach the Baltimore-Thurgood Marshall airport.
Some stations also link to Amtrak stations for rail service to other parts of the country. The Union Station, New Carrollton, Rockville, and King Street stations all have Amtrak stations.

8. Where is the Metro system located?
    a. Richmond
    b. Washington DC
    c. Baltimore
    d. Philadelphia

9. What types of vehicles are used in the Metro system?
    a. Buses
    b. Trolleys
    c. Taxis
    d. Rail cars

10. What makes the Union Station stop on the Metro distinct?
    a. This station moves to different lines
    b. The station offers an Amtrak hub
    c. You can get to an airport from Union Station
    d. Multiple platforms are included here

11. Which airport is directly linked to the Metro system?
    a. Washington-Ronald Reagan
    b. Washington-Dulles
    c. Baltimore-Thurgood Marshall
    d. All of these are linked to the system

12. What would you have to do when getting off at a train stop if you want to reach a different train on another line?
    a. See that the station serves that line in question
    b. Review which platform you have to be on
    c. Review the Amtrak connection
    d. A and B

13. Which of these stations is linked to the Amtrak system?
    a. King Street
    b. Fort Totten
    c. Rosslyn
    d. L'Enfant Plaza

14. How many lines are used in the Metro system?
    a. Four
    b. Five
    c. Six
    d. Seven

The following passage is to be used for Questions 15-23:

Conditions this Friday are expected to be 50 degrees with winds of 13 mph from the north-northeast. There is an elevated risk of rain at night with a 70 percent chance of rain. The chance of rain is reduced to 10 percent in the daytime. Expect a low of 42 degrees.

Saturday will be slightly warmer at 56 degrees with a low of 45. The wind remains at the north-northeast but will be 6 mph. There is a 40 percent chance of rain in the morning, but that should be the only time of the day when rain is likely to occur at.

The conditions on Sunday are dry with a high of 66 degrees and a low of 46. Winds are expected to be calm and will increase to 5 mph to the south, although they may pick up to around 10 mph during the evening. The winds should stay in the same direction throughout the day. There is a 10 percent chance of rain on

Sunday, although current radar patterns suggest that there will be no rain patterns making their way to the area until at least Wednesday.

15. How many days are covered in this passage?
    a. 1
    b. 2
    c. 3
    d. 4

16. What is not covered in the passage?
    a. Humidity
    b. Rain
    c. Wind
    d. Temperature

17. What day will be the warmest?
    a. Friday
    b. Saturday
    c. Sunday
    d. Monday

18. The chance for rain on Sunday is:
    a. 0 percent
    b. 10 percent
    c. 40 percent
    d. 70 percent

19. What will happen with the wind conditions on Sunday?
    a. They will change direction
    b. Hardly anything will be felt
    c. They will slightly pick up at night
    d. Conditions will get to 20 mph or higher

20. Which day has the largest difference between the high and the low for the day?
    a. Friday
    b. Saturday
    c. Sunday
    d. A and B

21. The largest chance for rain will occur on:
    a. Friday
    b. Saturday
    c. Sunday
    d. A and B

22. What can be said about the lows throughout the weekend?
    a. The lows will increase during the weekend
    b. The lows will drop
    c. The lows will stay the same
    d. The weather conditions will fluctuate throughout the weekend

23. What could potentially happen on Saturday morning?
    a. Rain
    b. Heat
    c. Cold
    d. Wind

The following passage is to be used for Questions 24-32:

The greatest concern in aviation activities is the possibility of fatigue. It becomes easy for people to become unable to focus if they are fatigued. If a person has been awake for a long period, they may not be able to concentrate fully on certain aspects of the job or react quickly to certain situations. By not being able to focus, it becomes harder for a person to stay alert.

The risk of fatigue can become more prevalent if a person has been working for too long without enough sleep. It is best for a person to have about 7 to 9 hours of sleep in one night if possible.

The best thing for a person to do to avoid fatigue is to have a sensible sleep schedule. This includes going to bed at or around the same time every night and then to wake up at or around the same time in the morning.

It is sensible for people to have some rest in the middle of the day. As useful as a nap may be, the risk of spending too much time napping can be great. There is always a potential that a 20-minute nap could end up being a 60-minute affair. Therefore, keeping a better sleep schedule at night is best when aiming to keep fatigue under control.

It is also smart to careful when contemplating overtime. Avoid working for any longer than what is normally required in the day if possible. Overtime can result in excess fatigue due to having exhausted their mental faculties during a long day of work.

Proper nutrition may also help to keep fatigue from being a threat. This includes having proper meals throughout the day and consuming enough water. Although caffeine-based drinks may be useful in some situations, such drinks may increase a person's likelihood to experience substantial weakness in the later part of the day after such a product's effect wears off. Following a more traditional approach to one's diet and nutrition is the best solution to avoid fatigue.

24. Who is this passage geared toward?
    a. Office workers
    b. Athletes
    c. Students
    d. Air pilots

25. Does the passage frown upon the consumption of caffeine-based drinks?
    a. At all times
    b. Not all the way
    c. Depends on your diet
    d. Depends on how much you need to do

26. What is the greatest problem with taking a nap in the middle of the day?
    a. It doesn't restore fatigue all that well
    b. The nap could last much longer than planned
    c. It may disrupt your schedule
    d. A person may become too tired after the rest is finished

27. The passage states that it helps to have a consistent sleep schedule. How many hours of sleep should a person have?
    a. Seven
    b. Eight
    c. Nine
    d. All of the above

28. What is the greatest risk of consuming caffeine according to the passage?
    a. Disruption to your sleep pattern
    b. Wear on your body
    c. You may experience more fatigue late in the day
    d. All of the above

29. Is it a good idea to work overtime?
    a. At all times
    b. Not at all
    c. Only in emergencies
    d. Talk with an officer for details

30. What reason does the passage give for avoiding fatigue?
    a. To be more alert on the job
    b. To lose weight
    c. To continue to work for as long as possible
    d. To manage time well enough

31. The passage says that the greatest concern about having a nap in the middle of the day is:
    a. The person not feeling rested
    b. Disturbances that can come along when trying to rest
    c. The nap lasting longer than expected
    d. How much work comes with trying to get to sleep

32. What should be done for one's diet according to the passage?
    a. Focus on a traditional approach to food
    b. Cut out fiber
    c. Keep sugar under control
    d. Allow for sugar early in the day if possible

The following passage is to be used for Questions 33-40:

An electronic keyboard will include several points for your convenience. First, the keyboard can include a full 88-key layout. The design is made to simulate the keys on a traditional keyboard. The arrangement of the keys should be sensible so you can reach them without experiencing problems.

Various setups can also be used on this electronic keyboard. These setups may include simulating particular instruments. In most cases, this will include different traditional piano-like instruments. Some panel effects may also be produced on an electronic keyboard, although you might need to get a separate attachment applied to the bottom part of the keyboard stand.

The buttons on the top part of an electronic keyboard will allow you to switch between setups and sounds. You may also produce some backing tracks on your keyboard, although that would require extra effort and some practice to produce the best possible tracks. You may also save some of these tracks and use them later if you are confident in what you have produced.

33. The keyboard should have how many keys?
    a. 44
    b. 66
    c. 88
    d. 15

34. The keyboard simulates what feature on a piano?
    a. Tones
    b. Pedals
    c. Effects
    d. Scales

35. The buttons on the top area can work with the following:
    a. Produce backing tracks
    b. Speed up sounds
    c. Activate microphone controls
    d. All of the above

36. What is the general idea of this passage?
    a. To explain what features are on an electronic keyboard
    b. To compare the electronic keyboard with other similar models
    c. To explain how to specifically use the electronic keyboard
    d. None of the above

37. What types of instruments can be simulated according to the reading?
    a. Woodwind instruments
    b. Drum beats
    c. Other piano-like instruments
    d. Vocal commands

38. What can be said about the passage?
    a. This may work as an advertisement
    b. This could be used in an instructional brochure
    c. The work explains to people how such an instrument works
    d. All of the above

39. How many tracks can be produced by the keyboard?
    a. As many as desired
    b. About 2 or 3 at a time
    c. You can only use one
    d. No specification in the passage

40. Who would benefit from this passage the most?
    a. A music instructor
    b. A music student
    c. A recording studio
    d. All of the above

The following passage is to be used for Questions 41-48:

Cincinnati-style chili is a popular entrée that features chili with unique spices and added ingredients served over hot spaghetti noodles. The recipe is served in hundreds of chili parlors around Cincinnati, but you don't have to travel to the Queen City to make Cincinnati-style chili on your own. You can prepare your own following a few steps.

You'll need to gather the needed seasonings. Cinnamon, allspice, nutmeg, oregano, and paprika are important to add to the recipe. Cocoa powder may also be added if desired, although it is not essential.

First, cook tomato paste by heating it in a pot – you will need about 3 ounces of tomato paste for every pound of beef. Add ground beef to the hot tomato paste and add a few cups of water. A good rule of thumb is to use one cup of water for every half-pound of ground beef that you are using.

Next, you will need to add the spices listed earlier. You can also add a tablespoon of vinegar to the recipe, with apple cider vinegar being one of the better options.

The mixture should be simmered uncovered for about 2 to 3 hours. A slow cooker is ideal to use. Stir often to ensure the chili is mixed well. You can let this simmer longer if desired.

You also have the option to cool the chili and then warm it again. If you notice some solidified bits of fat on the top part of the cooled chili, remove the fat and then reheat.

Be sure to cook the spaghetti according to the instructions on the package. Pour the finished chili on top of the drained spaghetti and serve.

You could also add red kidney beans that have been drained to the tomato sauce when it is finished cooking. Do not fix the beans to the chili until the very end. You can also sprinkle finely shredded cheddar cheese to the top of each dish. Minced yellow onions can also be added to the sauce as it is cooking. Don't forget to serve oyster crackers with the meal.

41. Which of these is not included in the recipe?
    a. Nutmeg
    b. Cocoa powder
    c. Allspice
    d. Cayenne pepper

42. Which ingredient is to be prepared first?
    a. Beans
    b. Tomato paste
    c. Ground beef
    d. Cheese

43. If you were to have 3 pounds of ground beef, how many cups of water would you have to add to the recipe?
    a. 3
    b. 4
    c. 5
    d. 6

44. What type of vinegar is recommended?
    a. Balsamic
    b. Malt
    c. Apple Cider
    d. Rice

45. What should be done with the kidney beans?
    a. Add at the end
    b. Drain everything
    c. Use red beans
    d. All of the above

46. How many hours does the recipe say that you would have to heat the chili?
    a. 1 hour
    b. 2 hours
    c. 5 hours
    d. 10 hours

47. When would you notice solid bits of fat in your recipe?
    a. When you chill the recipe
    b. When you heat it too much
    c. When you add lots of vinegar
    d. When you add beans

48. What does the writer say about cocoa powder in the recipe?
    a. You must use it
    b. Do not use it
    c. You can use it if you wish
    d. The sugar content should be checked first

The following passage is to be used for Questions 49-52:

The stock is currently trading at 50. The stock has experienced a number of changes in the past year. The stock started the year at 47, and eventually went up to 55. Since then, the stock has not experienced any sizable ups or downs. The changes in the value appear to be gradual without any dramatic shifts.

49. The stock's value is:
    a. 47
    b. 50
    c. 55
    d. 58

50. What was the highest value of the stock in the past year?
    a. 47
    b. 50
    c. 55
    d. 58

51. How long is the stock report for?
    a. In the past 12 months
    b. In the last month
    c. For a few years
    d. Since the start of the year

52. What type of analysis is used in this paragraph?
    a. A prospectus for the stock to move up or down after a while
    b. How much the stock is going up or down at a time
    c. The general range of the stock
    d. Shift in the stock's value

The following passage is to be used for Questions 53-56:

The umpire has discretion to eject players from a baseball game as they see fit. The umpire could eject a person because of actions, such as questioning calls, attempting to harm other players, or acting in a retaliatory way. The history between teams or players may also be considered as a team that has dealt with significant problems with another team could possibly retaliate or the situation could erupt in violence. The umpire will have to review how these teams are functioning and what might happen when playing against each other.

53. The passage is about:
    a. Football
    b. Soccer
    c. Baseball
    d. Cricket

54. What does the passage state about the impact of a game?
    a. An umpire can decide when to eject players
    b. The umpire has control over balls and strikes
    c. Players can dispute calls if they wish
    d. All of the above

55. What can be said about the analysis of players?
    a. Players may be judgmental
    b. Players are hard to control
    c. Not all players are going to work with the rules of the game
    d. Players between teams may have hostile attitudes toward one another

56. Why would baseball players on other teams become abusive toward one another according to the paragraph?
    a. Competitive advantage
    b. Personal concerns
    c. Image issues
    d. Retaliation

Reading Comprehension Answers

1. a. The entire passage focuses on a convention center. The meeting room and mezzanine are parts of the convention center that are both discussed.

2. b. The language of the passage gives the impression that a person who operates a business could benefit from having one's business participate in activities supported by the convention center.

3. a. B is not the correct answer in that it refers to the main exhibit hall area, not the ballroom.

4. b. The exhibit hall takes up 200,000 square feet that is 500,000 square feet in size.

5. b. The mezzanine is directly linked to a hotel.

6. d. None of the other options are mentioned in the passage.

7. d. The passage says that up to 700 vendors can be accommodated by the exhibit hall. Therefore, all 3 of the other options are correct.

8. b. The passage is about the public transit rail system that operates in Washington DC.

9. d. The passage specifically states that the Metro is a series of rail cars moving along set lines.

10. b. You can reach Amtrak through Union Station, but you must reach another station to reach the airport.

11. a. While the Reagan airport is linked to the Metro through a dedicated station, you would have to go to other specific stations and then take a certain bus route to reach the Dulles or Marshall airports.

12. d. The passage states that many stops serve multiple lines, but multiple platforms may also be used depending on where you are.

13. a. B refers to a station that links many lines. The other 2 choices are places that connect to airports through bus route transfers. A is the only valid option.

14. c. The first paragraph states there are 6 lines.

15. c. Friday, Saturday, and Sunday are all covered in this passage.

16. a. There are no defining or definite features in the paragraph that mention humidity.

17. c. The first sentences of each paragraph list the highs for the day.

18. b. The chance for rain on Sunday is at 10 percent.

19. c. The paragraph for Sunday states that the wind will pick up by a small amount during the evening hours.

20. c. There is a 20-degree differential between the high and low on Sunday. That number is 8 on Friday and 11 on Saturday.

21. a. Friday's forecast states that there is a 70 percent chance of rain, which is the largest chance for the weekend.

22. a. The lows increase each day according to the passage.

23. a. The morning is the time of the day when rain is more likely to occur.

24. d. The first paragraph specifically states that the passage explains the need of air pilots to have enough sleep.

25. b. The writer is not shunning such drinks, but it is critical for a person to be cautious.

26. b. The passage states that a person could have an extended nap instead of a short one.

27. d. The passage cites that having 7 to 9 hours of rest every night is the best thing to do.

28. c. The passage does not state anything suggesting that your sleep pattern could be disrupted, although there is a chance that such a concern may occur.

29. b. Fatigue can occur during overtime hours. The best thing to do in this situation is to avoid working overtime to keep the possible fatigue of working overtime from being a threat.

30. a. The implication is that a person needs to focus on being active and productive without risking any possible fatigue-related concerns.

31. c. There are often problems with a nap being much longer than intended.

32. a. The article suggests that people should consume food with control.

33. c. The 88-key layout is consistent with what would appear on a traditional keyboard.

34. d. Scales are simulated based on the things that can work in many situations.

35. a. This answer appears to be the only point that is introduced in this segment.

36. a. The features of the keyboard are described, but the passage does not go as far as to explain how one would actually use the said keyboard.

37. c. The work states that various piano instruments can be simulated through the instrument.

38. d. The instrument can produce unique sounds of different instruments.

39. d. Although the description states that many tracks can be produced, there is no information on specific tracks.

40. d. A person who needs something to record music or to perform it could benefit from the item.

41. d. Cayenne pepper is not mentioned in the recipe.

42. b. The tomato paste part of the recipe is the first to be prepared.

43. d. The passage states to add one cup of water for every half-pound of ground beef. Therefore, you would add 6 cups of water to 3 pounds of beef.

44. c. Apple cider vinegar is the only one specifically mentioned in the recipe.

45. d. Each of these options is listed.

46. b. The recipe states to heat it for 2 to 3 hours.

47. a. The passage states that the recipe can be chilled and simmered later. But when you chill the recipe, solidified bits of fat may potentially develop on the surface. These would have to be removed.

48. c. Cocoa powder is an option.

49. b. The stock value is 50 at the beginning.

50. c. The highest value of the stock is 55 based on the current year.

51. d. The stock report states that the stock was at 47 at the beginning of the year. This means that the passage has covered points on a stock's value since the beginning of the current year.

52. b. There are no predictive comments in the paragraph.

53. c. The first sentence specifically states that the passage is about baseball.

54. a. The passage is about the umpire's ability to eject players in a baseball game.

55. d. Players may engage in rough behavior toward people on other teams.

56. d. Retaliation often occurs when people engage in actions that are designed to respond to certain things that happened in the past.

Chapter 9 – Situational Judgment

Any job requires people to take quick, decisive actions, and the Air Force is no exception. The situational judgment subtest is designed to assess how well you make such decisions.

The situational judgment questions describe a hypothetical problem that you will have to solve. You must look at the situation, consider the five possible options given and select the most effective, appropriate solution.

Keys for Answering Questions

When answering the questions in the situational judgment segment of the AFOQT exam, ask yourself:

1. What could be the possible consequences of the decision you choose to make?

Consider what will happen as a result of your decision and whether any problems or repercussions could result.

2. How would other people be impacted by the choices you make?

Look at how other people will be influenced by your decision.

3. Is your decision ethical or sensible?

Some decisions you make could be against the law or immoral.

4. Is your decision really necessary?

Just because you *can* do something doesn't mean you actually should do it.

Situational Judgment Questions

Note: The questions in this segment are organized with 2 questions in mind. For the first question for a situation, you will have to choose which of the 5 possible answers would be appropriate. For the second question, you must list which of the other 4 answers is the least appropriate for the situation. Be aware of the time you have for answering the questions and that you note all the scenarios at hand.

1-2. You find 10 new boxes that have been loaded in the stock room. Half of those boxes have not been entered into the computer program used to keep a record for the items received. A subordinate is supposed to take care of these shipments as they come in. The key is to ensure that the items are scanned as soon as they come in.

    a. Scan the items on your own. Tell someone else, particularly a senior officer that you are having a problem with the person who is supposed to be doing this job.

    b. Scan the items on your own without telling anyone about the issue.

    c. Tell subordinates about what they should be doing and that they should be scanning these items.

    d. Write a note telling your subordinates to scan the items when they get a chance.

    e. Criticize the subordinate for not doing their work at the right time.

3-4. A couple of men in the field are harassing a woman in the Air Force on social media. They are intimidating and mocking her, and nothing is sexual in nature. However, it appears as though her confidence is being impacted.

    a. Talk with the men who are harassing the woman and let them know that their actions will be reported if they do not stop what they are doing.

    b. Go to the woman in question and provide support for her. You can tell her that you want to talk with the men who are harassing her, but you should not do this unless she says she agrees.

    c. Provide support for the woman, and let her know that she needs to report the situation and that you can do this if she is unable to or does not want to.

    d. Talk with your superior about the concern.

    e. Do nothing about it. The problem should resolve itself on its own, and you do not know what someone wants.

5-6. You have been dealing with serious problems regarding another person in the field. You are being told that you have to do a job with him, but you are not comfortable about this. You feel it is impossible to work with him.

  a. Let another person who is interested in working with this person take care of the task.
  b. Provide the position to someone who is suited to handle the situation.
  c. Give the role to someone else at random.
  d. Complete the task as requested.
  e. Ask another team member about what should be done to reassign the role.

7-8. You are on a team where one of the members is from a different part of the world and has a culture that is much different from what you are used to. That foreign person regularly uses a word that is often considered to be a slur in your culture. You are uncertain as to whether that person thinks that the word has a completely different meaning in their culture or if that person is intentionally insulting you.

  a. Tell your superior officer about how this person is using the objectionable word.
  b. Tell your team members to stop using the word.
  c. Talk with other people on your team about how the word is being used.
  d. Tell the people on the team that the word means something different to you and that the word should no longer be used.
  e. Do nothing, as you might be accused of being culturally insensitive.

9-10. You are working in a new unit that does not have enough staff members. The group has been bearing with extensive scheduling and administrative issues that are keeping the unit from being as effective as it should be. However, you are only going to be in that unit for about 2 months, but you have worries as to what you are supposed to do in this particular situation. You need to decide if there is something you can do about the situation even if your concerns are going to be short-lived.

  a. Don't bother doing anything.
  b. Tell the people in charge that you will need extra help.
  c. Copy what the people on your team are doing.
  d. Ask the administrative team for help or clarification about what you should do.
  e. Don't put in much effort. You might have hopes of getting out of the unit earlier.

11-12. You are going to be taking care of a very important visitor. You are arranging for a conference room to use. However, you notice that there is another meeting taking place in the room that you have chosen. You see that people are setting up for that meeting and you want to know what event is planned. They tell you that they are setting up the conference room for a particular event.

    a. State that you were not aware that the room was being used at the time (even though you might have known this earlier).
    b. Let the other team know that they have to find another space for their meeting.
    c. Ask the director about the situation and ask if there are possible alternative spaces for a meeting.
    d. Talk with the people at the room about what is at stake, and listen to their situation and what is at stake for them as well.
    e. Reschedule your meeting for the room for some other time.

13-14. You are interviewing 2 separate people for a position. The first candidate appears to be suitable for the position. The second candidate is a friend of your superior, and while that person has talent, they may not necessarily be the best candidate. You are being asked by your superior about who should be hired.

    a. Say that you don't have an opinion.
    b. Do not answer the question, as you feel that your superior has probably made the decision already.
    c. Say that the second candidate is best because you know that's who the superior wants.
    d. Say that you want to work with new candidates to avoid a conflict of interest.
    e. Tell the superior that the first candidate has better qualifications.

15-16. You have been notified of new equipment that you desperately want to for your workplace. Your superior is listed as one of the people who are being considered to receive that new equipment, and you are not among the people on that list.

    a. Contact a subordinate and state that you need that equipment more than your superior does.
    b. Complain about the issue and ask to get your own equipment sent to you.
    c. Tell your superior officer that there has been a mistake that needs to be resolved and that you are not getting the equipment you need to complete your job.
    d. Demand your superior officer to arrange for you to receive the equipment you need.
    e. Say that you are going to transfer to a different unit that will provide you with the equipment that you need to do the job.

17-18. You have noticed that one of your subordinates is not doing the things he is supposed to be doing. He has developed a negative attitude about his work and is often missing deadlines. You are surprised about this as you have not had problems with him in the past and their work has usually been excellent.

    a. Tell your superior officer about the problem. Ask for advice on what should be done to handle the concern.
    b. Tell the subordinate that they will be terminated if their behavior does not change. You have to list an action plan surrounding what will happen if that person does not take care of the work properly.
    c. Tell the subordinate about how their behavior is negatively impacting the unit in general. Discuss what can be done to help them improve their performance.
    d. Ask the entire unit about what should be done. The goal should be to get the worker to recognize that he is causing harm and is not making things easier for everyone else.
    e. Do nothing and figure that your subordinate's behavior is going to change after a while.

19-20. One of your fellow workers has been changing some of the numbers on the reports you are reviewing. These numbers indicate how many people are required for particular tasks. You are concerned about this because you feel that by having those numbers changed, the success of the mission or task could be in jeopardy.

  a. Do nothing, because the person you are questioning understands what they are doing.
  b. Tell a superior officer that the numbers have been changed.
  c. Write a message to the worker and say that you know what is going on.
  d. Say that you will not work with that person until they admit to changing the numbers and modifying the information.
  e. Ask the worker for an explanation as to why the numbers were changed. You can also talk with a superior officer about the situation.

21-22. You are trying to keep account of the inventory in the office. However, you always notice that when one particular person comes along, something ends up being missing afterward. You might notice things missing like some items other bits of equipment that are necessary for certain tasks in your environment.

  a. Catch that person in the act. After that, you can take action.
  b. Do not do anything.
  c. Tell a superior officer that someone is stealing from your area.
  d. Tell the person that you know what they are doing. Ask for an explanation.
  e. Let your coworkers know about the situation, and have them all watch what is happening in the work environment.

23-24. You have been working on a certain project with another officer for the last few months. However, that officer has been absent often in the last few weeks. They have been ill in many cases. When that person does appear, you experience some frustration because they are not able to handle the work. You experience constant annoyance because you are constantly behind in your work as a result.

  a. Keep on working without complaining. This includes working with the added workload involved.
  b. Tell your superior that your work partner is not doing their job.
  c. Send an email to the absent partner when they are off sick. Talk about how frustrated you are that they are constantly absent.
  d. Ask your superior officer what should be done next, as your current situation is not going as well as you want.
  e. Do nothing and figure that the project is going to keep progressing.

25-26. The superior officer and general officer are both in the middle of an argument with one another. They are arguing about whether or not a new project in the workplace is worth starting. You don't see the general officer very often, but you see the superior officer almost every day. The general officer has the highest ranking of all the parties in the room. After the 2 are finished debating the affair, you are asked your opinion by these people about what should be done.

    a. Support the general officer because they have the highest rank of everyone in the room.
    b. Support the superior officer out of fear of what would happen if you did not.
    c. Decide what makes the 2 sides different from one another, and make a reasoned decision between the 2.
    d. Do not answer out of fear that you could get dragged into the ongoing dispute
    e. State your opinion about what can be done to resolve the problem between the 2 sides of the argument.

27-28. The general layout of your unit is not arranged as well as you wish it could be. You have designed a new organizational structure that would allow all parties to feel more comfortable with one another while providing a sensible layout. You told your coworkers about the new structure, and they all approve. However, the senior officer is not happy about the idea and feels that it might take weeks or even months for the work you want to do to be put into effect.

    a. Accept what the senior officer says.
    b. Produce a presentation that explains to the senior officer what you want to do. Be ready to accept the final decision that the officer makes based on your presentation.
    c. Keep the design you want to use in spite of what your officer says.
    d. Keep working on the current platform, but list various ways your new plan could be used to correct any problems that might happen.
    e. Let the senior officer know that the project has been approved by all the other people in the group.

29-30. You have been working on a project with a co-worker who has been working on the same tasks. Everyone in the project will have to complete the task simultaneously and provide enough help. However, a co-worker says that 2 of the team members are no longer partaking in the assignment for various reasons. You are being told by others that you have very specific things that have to be done in the work environment and that the extra help needs to be provided to take care of all the tasks.

 a. Do not help the co-worker who is causing the dispute because it is their fault the task is not working as well as it should.
 b. Look at what your co-worker needs to have accomplished and delegate the work among all team members.
 c. Meet with another officer to decide what to do to get the work done on time.
 d. Help the co-worker by allowing the work to be divided among many people.
 e. Let the co-worker know that you are sorry about what is happening and that you don't think the other people in the group should be held liable for whatever is happening.

31-32. You are going to assign particular tasks to 3 junior members. One of those junior members has directly said to you that they are hoping to get on one specific task. However, you were planning to have them work on another task. This is particularly a task that you feel that person would be better suited to complete.

 a. Give the position you were going to assign to the person who wants it.
 b. Give the position to whoever is best suited for the task.
 c. Assign the position at random to the 3 people. You could also allow the 3 to rotate between the tasks.
 d. Complete the task on your own instead.
 e. Have another person be asked about how the task should be assigned and if it should be done differently than what you were planning to do.

33-34. You noticed that one particular partner you are working with is making a mistake. You openly state that they are making the mistake, and you want to correct that problem. However, the partner becomes increasingly frustrated with you and yells at you to stop interfering. You tried to reason with him but they leave. That person has responded this way to criticism in the past.

    a. Wait for that person to come back and tell them to stop yelling.
    b. Do nothing because you do not want to make the arguments or conflicts worse.
    c. Ask other teammates whether they have witnessed reactions like this in the past.
    d. Tell your superior about that person's behavior.
    e. Avoid working with that person in the future.

35-36. You are about to get a promotion for your work in handling resources and in producing a more efficient group. However, you feel that your team is not doing as well with handling its workload as others. Also, you feel that your team has not been staffed as well as others.

    a. Be thankful for the promotion, but also explain that there are substantial issues in your work environment that still need to be resolved.
    b. Tell a superior officer about your concerns.
    c. Ask your team members about what they feel they should be doing for you.
    d. Do not do anything and wait to see how well your team continues to operate.
    e. Tell your superior that you are going to leave the team if the issues you have are not resolved soon.

37-38. You received an email from someone in your group, and that email appears to be inappropriate. You know that the email is not compliant with the communication standards you have imposed in the workplace.

    a. Send an email back to that person. Say that you are not happy with the message, but make sure the discipline is informal in nature.
    b. Forward the email to others and let them know that this is not how emails are to be sent in the workplace.
    c. Talk with that person about what should be done in the future regarding emails.
    d. Ask for advice from your superior officer about what you should do next.
    e. Remind your subordinates about email privileges in the workplace.

39-40. You are being asked to lead a few subordinates, but you are not clear as to what the mission is or what tasks have to be completed.

   a. Ask the supervisor who assigned you the task for further guidance.
   b. Ask the person who was previously assigned the task for help.
   c. Meet with the most senior subordinate to discuss the mission.
   d. Meet with each subordinate to get to know them better.
   e. Call a meeting and let all the subordinates know you need help.

41-42. You are running a project that is not directly under your supervision. The engineer is regularly providing updates, but the engineer often leaves out important facts.

   a. Talk during a meeting to express the concern on your own.
   b. Discuss your concerns with an engineer.
   c. Tell the engineer's supervisor about your concerns.
   d. Let the supervisor know you have concerns and that you are seeking outside advice.
   e. Have a private meeting with a commander to present all the information.

Situational Judgment Answers

1. c. Ensure that the subordinates are being told to do their jobs. Let the subordinate who is not doing something properly know about what has to be done.

2. b. A subordinate is supposed to take care of the task. More importantly, you need to ensure that anyone in the area is aware of what is happening and that a plan for scanning the items is in enforced.

3. b. You should let the woman in question know there is help for her and that she has the opportunity to resolve the situation. However, you should only provide this help if she is willing to take it. The woman has the right to make the choice.

4. e. Something has to be done about the situation before it is worse. Someone has to be consulted.

5. e. Another person in your team should be consulted about the event and what may be done to resolve the problem.

6. c. You should not try to let just anyone take your position. If you were to give your position to someone else (which in itself may not be the best idea), you would have to instead give it to a person who has actual experience in a situation and understands what can be done to resolve an issue.

7. d. You have to explain to the person in question about what the word means to you and that it is offensive to you.

8. e. You will need to talk with the team member about the issue and how it is creating a problem for you. Not doing anything about the situation will make the problem worse.

9. d. You probably have no knowledge as to what you should do in this situation. You can talk with an administrative person about what should be done to resolve the issue.

10. e. Intentionally performing poorly will make it harder for people to trust you and feel that you are doing things properly.

11. d. The best thing to do is to get on the same page as the other party in the room. Talk about what is happening and decide which team needs the conference area more.

12. a. This is the least appropriate thing you could do because it will negatively reflect upon your behavior.

13. e. You have to let the superior know that the first person is definitely the best choice regardless of any personal wishes of the superior. The superior should be aware of the best choice for the benefit of the business.

14. c. You should not try to make decisions based on what someone wants even if it is not the correct choice to make. You must consider what would be the most beneficial thing to do.

15. c. There is a chance that the concern was an unintentional mistake and that the problem can be resolved with a simple discussion.

16. e. You are likely to cause an unnecessary conflict if you threaten something like this. The conflict would cause the situation to become worse than it needs to be.

17. c. A careful discussion with the person who is causing the problems can help identify what should be done to find a resolution.

18. e. There is a chance that the subordinate's behavior will become worse, so talk with that person as soon as possible to resolve the problems.

19. e. You need to talk with the worker about what is happening and that there is clearly something wrong. This includes looking at any possible things that could be done to correct the issues before they become worse.

20. a. You have to put in an effort to determine what is working. In other words, you cannot afford to stop working.

21. d. You need to get a direct explanation from the person about what is happening. If they continue to ignore you or refuse to come clean, you might need to produce some evidence confirming what you have noticed.

22. b. There is a chance that the losses will continue if you did not do something. You must take action as soon as possible.

23. d. Your officer should be the one to tell you what to do next. You should not try to sneak around your partner's work. You can especially use the services of an officer to confirm something that you want to do with the work you are planning.

24. e. You are probably doing your share of the work at this point. Not letting the other person do the same would only make it harder for your task to be completed.

25. c. The choice you make should not be based on pressure from others. The choice should be based on what you feel would be appropriate for all parties. Be sure you review the choice that you want to make and that the option suits the needs of all people involved.

26. d. You have to provide some answer to the people in this situation. Do not stay quiet, or else people will feel that you are not reliable or capable to handle the issue.

27. b. Your presentation does not have to be elaborate. You only need to let that person know about your plans that would make it effective.

28. c. The problem with what you are actively doing right now is that it might not be effective. You need to provide extra details on how your proposed idea would work well.

29. d. Allow the work to be divided between multiple people. You need plenty of people to be on hand to help you and identify new opportunities for work.

30. a. The person who is not doing well should be assisted in some way. This includes looking at possible ways to make it easier for tasks to be completed.

31. b. Whoever is capable of doing things the best should be consulted. Be ready to allow that person to think about what is working and how they can handle the job.

32. e. You should be the one responsible for making the decisions regarding situations like this, and not someone else who might not be prepared.

33. d. A superior officer should help you identify what can be done to fix the problem and to keep it from being a threat to others in the future.

34. e. There is no way to choose which people you are going to work with in most cases, so the best thing you could do would be to resolve the problem and to talk with the person in question about what should be done to correct the issue.

35. b. You have to let an officer know that while you are putting in hard work, you need help. You have to be honest when talking about what is happening in your work environment.

36. d. Failing to do something will make the situation worse. Your team members may also stop trusting you.

37. c. A direct talk with the person who sent the inappropriate email can let them know what should be done to resolve problems and to keep these issues from being any worse in the future.

38. b. Forwarding that email to other people would be akin to embarrassing or shaming that person responsible. This could make it harder for people to trust you and feel comfortable with working with you for fear that you might do the same to them.

39. c. The most senior member of the group may give you additional ideas on what to do.

40. a. Talking with the supervisor about the task might make it harder for you to get an answer or to be trusted.

41. b. You can talk directly with an engineer in a meeting to get an idea of what might be working in your situation.

42. e. Talking with a commander about the issues might make it harder for you to be taken seriously.

Chapter 10 – Science: Chemistry

Science is a cornerstone of the world of aviation. This chapter concentrates on various aspects pertaining to science, such as chemistry and physics, and how these may be applied on the job. Some of the content in this subtest is highly technical in nature.

The periodic table of elements identifies the different elements and denotes their unique relationship to one another. The periodic table can be found later in this chapter.

Atoms and Chemical Elements

The chemical elements are atoms that have the same number of protons in their nuclei. There are 118 of these elements that have been identified and listed on the periodic table of elements.

The atoms have been identified based on Niels Bohr's model:

1. Protons – positively charged ions found in the nucleus

2. Neutrons – neutrally charged ions found in the nucleus

3. Electrons – negatively charged ions surrounding the nucleus

The elements are organized on a periodic table based on their atomic numbers, which equal the number of protons in the nucleus. Protons determine the chemical properties within an element.

The atomic mass is also noted, as elements with a higher number of protons will have a greater atomic mass. The mass is a measure of the size of an element based on atomic mass units or amu. The amu is equal to the approximate number of protons or neutrons in an atom, or the average number based on how different isotopes (forms of an element with the same number of protons but different numbers of neutrons) may be incorporated in the measurement.

An example of this may be noticed with lithium, listed on the chart as Li. Lithium has an atomic number of 3 and an atomic mass of 6.94. This means that there are three protons in an atom of lithium, and the protons and neutrons combine for an average mass of 6.94 amu. Lead or Pb has an atomic number of 82 and an atomic mass of 207.2, indicating that lead is a larger, heavier element.

Chemical Reactions

When a series of chemicals (referred to as reactants) come in contact with each other, changes occur in the molecular structures of the atoms. The product of this reaction is new chemicals. The bonds that link atoms will change, while the nuclei do not.

There are four types of chemical reactions. Each of these types is different based on what occurs when certain elements combine with one another.

1. Combination

A combination reaction occurs when reactants combine to create a larger and more complex substance. The bonds in the reactants break, and new bonds are produced to create different reactions. A good example of this iron and chromium. When these two elements mix with one another, the combination reaction produces ferrochrome, an alloy of iron and chromium.

2. Decomposition

Decomposition involves two chemicals combining in a destructive fashion. One chemical breaks down into other products. The atomic bonds of that chemical break and are rearranged into a new configuration. An example of decomposition is when water is subjected to electrolysis and produces the gases hydrogen and oxygen. The hydrogen and oxygen then break down and trigger the decomposition process.

3. Combustion

Combustion occurs when oxygen is a reactant. This occurs, for instance, when fuel is burned (such as in an engine) and oxygen is released in the process.

4. Oxidation

Oxidation occurs when oxygen is transferred between elements, either weakening or strengthening the product of the chemical reaction. Outside sources may influence the extent of the reaction. The pathway of the reaction may include a catalyst.

Oxidation numbers can be assigned to a chemical compound, indicating the impact of the oxygen in the compound. The combination will be neutral (noted as 0), or a positive or negative change.

Chemical Structure and Reading a Chemical Formula

A chemical's structure is based on the layout of individual atoms and their bonds.

A chemical formula denotes how atoms are structurally arranged. For example, C_2H_6O (ethanol) has a combination of carbon, hydrogen and oxygen. The equation denotes the presences of two carbon atoms, six hydrogen atoms and one oxygen atom.

The layout of C_2H_6O suggests that, structurally, carbon will have the greatest impact on in this chemical formula.

Stoichiometry

Stoichiometry is a branch of chemistry that focuses on the strong relationships between reactants in a chemical reaction. The impact of certain chemicals can influence a chemical's potency. Stoichiometry is used to determine the ratios of the reactants that appear in a chemical reaction.

In a stoichiometric process, the molar mass of each element must be obtained by consulting the periodic table. Each element has a different molar mass based upon the weight of said element's atoms. For instance, boron has a molar mass of 10.81 g/mol, and nitrogen has a molar mass of 14.007 g/mol.

To calculate molecular weight, multiply the number of atoms of an element by the element's molar mass. For instance, to find H_3N_2F's molecular mass, do the following:

H_3 = 1.01 (molar mass) x 3 (number of atoms) = 3.03

N_2 = 14.007 x 2 = 28.014

F = 18.998

Total molecular mass: 50.042

You can also determine the percentage each individual element contributes to the entire mass. For hydrogen: divide 3.03 by 50.042. This amounts to 6.1% of the total mass; for nitrogen: divide 28.014 by 50.042. This amounts to 56% of the total mass of the solution.

You can use these totals for when you need to balance equations. For instance, you might need to balance 2 C_2O_2 + 3 H_2O. For 2 C_2O_2, you have two parts of that particular element with a total mass of 112.04 and the second element of 3 H_2O has a mass of 54.045. In order to balance the equation, more components of H_2O are needed. You may need three more of the H_2O compounds in order to create a balance.

Isotopes and their Relationship in Nuclear Functions

Isotopes are forms of an element that contain the same number of protons but different numbers of neutrons. Isotopes are significant because they can cause an element to become unstable depending on the number of isotopes present. Though it's difficult to determine when isotopes are going to break down, the half-life of an isotope can be measured based on how long it takes for the nuclei in atoms to break down through radioactive decay. When an isotope is unstable and experiences a sizable amount of decay, the material may become dangerous and need to be isolated.

There are three types of radioactive decay:

1. Alpha

Alpha decay is when an atom emits two protons and two neutrons from the nucleus, triggering the creation of a new element in many situations. This usually occurs in larger elements. The radiation emitted is very weak.

2. Beta

Beta decay occurs when an electron is emitted from the neutron of an atom. As a result, the electron count increases. When a new element is produced, beta radiation occurs and is stronger than alpha radiation. However, many heavy materials, such as wood, can block beta radiation.

3. Gamma

Gamma decay occurs when a substance's atomic mass increases. The charge on the atom doesn't change. Rather, the element breaks down and produces harmful gamma radiation. This radiation is powerful and can only be blocked by lead. The lead material may also be dangerous if not handled properly.

Critical Isotopes

It is never easy to predict what might happen during the creation of an isotope. Radium, actinium and uranium can decay into other elements depending on their isotopes.

The decay chain of an element can be dictated by the isotope. Uranium Z or ^{234}Pa is an example; it is an isotope of protactinium that appears in the decay chain of uranium; ^{212}Bi is an isotope of bismuth that occurs from the decay of thorium; ^{212}Po is an isotope of polonium formed by the decay of thorium. These isotopes are dictated by their atomic weights and other critical properties.

pH Scale

The pH scale, measured on a scale from 0 to 14, is used to review how basic or acidic a water-based material is. pH level is a reference to the power of hydrogen in a compound. A pH of seven is considered neutral. A lower pH level (anything under six) means that a substance is acidic, and this means that it can donate a proton to another and produce a covalent bond through an electron pair. A higher pH level (anything over seven) means that the substance is a base and can accept protons.

You can tell that an element combination is acidic if an H appears at the start of the formula. On the other hand, a base contains OH at the end of its signature.

Some common bases include bleach, baking soda, ammonia and seawater. Common acids include battery acid, lemon juice, vinegar, tomato juice and black coffee.

Periodic Table

The periodic table, created in 1869 by Dmitri Mendeleev, is a critical aspect of chemistry as it organizes elements in nature based on their properties such as what elements are alike and their size. As elements are discovered, they are added to the table.

There are more than a hundred different elements listed on the periodic table. Each element is labeled: the atomic number is at the top and is a reference to the number of protons in an atom of the element; a one or two-letter symbol for the element; the atomic mass of the element. The number of electrons in each shell of an atom may also be noted at the bottom of an element's individual square, but are not always included.

The elements are aligned in columns by similar properties.

Take note of the following element groupings in the periodic table:

1. Alkali metals

The alkali metals are in the first column of the table with hydrogen being the exception. Lithium, sodium, potassium, rubidium, cesium and francium are all metals that have the outermost electron in an s-orbital. This means that there is a shared configuration of electrons. Each of these metals is soft and can be easily cut.

2. Alkaline earth metals

Alkaline earth metals, found in the second column, include beryllium, magnesium, calcium, strontium, barium and radium. These metals are noted for being shiny and having a white-like appearance. They have common s-electron shells, each with two electrons. These appear in nature for the most part, though radium is produced not by natural effects but rather from the decay of uranium and thorium. As a result, it is extremely difficult to produce the metal.

3. Transition metals

Transition metals are found throughout much of the middle part of the periodic table. A transition metal has a partially filled sub-shell that can create additional reactions. The elements from columns 3 to 12 are all transition metals. The qualities of each metal are different based on atomic number, mass and other factors. (Note: Mercury is listed as a transition metal, although the highly hazardous and toxic material is naturally found as a liquid. However, the chemical properties of mercury are similar to those of many transition metals, although mercury itself is highly unstable.)

4. Post-transition metals

A post-transition metal is one that can produce covalent bonds. These are often soft or brittle. These metals have low melting points and weak mechanical strengths. They elements appear in row 13 at the beginning and progress to the bottom part of the table. Common post-transition metals include aluminum, indium, tin, lead, bismuth and polonium.

5. Metalloids

A metalloid is a metal that has properties of both metal and nonmetal elements. The material has a metallic look, but the compound is not a good conductor of electricity. Metalloids are brittle, making it difficult for them to be utilized for many structures. There are seven metalloids on the table: boron, silicon, germanium, arsenic, antimony, tellurium and astatine. Aluminum and carbon can be interpreted as metalloids because of their chemical properties, but these are not necessarily metalloids due to how they may be prepared in many forms with more reinforced bodies that are easier to handle in many construction and production situations.

6. Nonmetals

Nonmetals are made of different compounds and are more natural in arrangement. These are found around the right end of the periodic table. A few solids are included like carbon, phosphorous, sulfur, selenium and iodine. These elements are very fragile. Nitrogen, oxygen, fluorine and chlorine are nonmetal gases, while bromine is a liquid included in this section. (Note: Bromine and mercury are the only two liquids in the table.)

7. Noble gases

Noble gases are found in the final column at the far right section of the periodic table. A noble gas is odorless, colorless and will not react to chemicals. The noble gases are helium, neon, argon, krypton, xenon and radon. These gases can be used for many purposes including producing light. Noble gases generally produce no radiation, although radon may display some radioactive properties depending on how the element is produced.

8. Unknown elements

The elements from atomic number 104 to 118 are unknown. These are elements that may be produced as synthetic materials, but it is unclear how they behave. Many of these synthetic elements are often dangerous to produce and may come in solid, liquid or gas forms. These elements are named mainly based on their atomic numbers and how they are constructed.

The features of each of these unknown elements are varied, but they can be dangerous. Rutherfordium is a good example, as this element is highly radioactive. Copernicium is an element that has an extremely short life and is also radioactive. Oganesson is considered to be a gas, although it is uncertain how stable the gas may be.

9. Lanthanoids and actinoids

You may notice two columns in the periodic table that are separate from the others. The first row features lanthanoids. These metallic elements, atomic numbers 57 to 71, are considered to be rare earth elements. The elements are similar to lanthanum and include items like ytterbium and erbium. Such elements are likely to develop when they chemically combine with other elements. Further research is required to identify how these elements behave and what makes them function.

Actinoids, atomic numbers 89 to 103, are on the bottom row, starting with actinium. The most important characteristic of these elements is that they are extremely radioactive and may be dangerous if not handled properly. Such elements include curium, americium, polonium and thorium. These elements are man-made and should be monitored carefully due to how unpredictable they are.

You need to know the symbols for each of the elements. The symbols are often named based on the official names of these elements, although there may be some differences due to the Greek and Latin terms often used. Lithium has the symbol Li from the Greek word lithos. Helium has He symbol from the Greek word Helios.

In other cases, a completely different series of letters will be used for different elements. Potassium is represented by a K from the Latin word kalium. Antimony has the symbol Sb from the Latin word stibnite. Gold has Au as its symbol from the Latin word aurum.

The Future of the Periodic Table

Right now, the highest value of an element on the periodic table is 118. This is for oganesson, an element whose final form is not clearly known. As there are many elements that have yet to be discovered or formulated, the possibility exists that the periodic table will continue to grow.

Undiscovered elements may appear on a table beyond the 118 atomic number. Such elements will feature symbols with three letters, with the symbols starting with a U. These elements are considered synthetic. The lightest of these future elements is at periodic number 119, ununennium or Uue. The element is anticipated to be an alkali metal and is expected to have properties similar to lithium, sodium and others on the left end of the periodic table. However, general efforts to try and mix elements like calcium and einsteinium together have proven to be unsuccessful.

Additional Symbols

Pictographic symbols are symbols of elements that have been used since the early days of alchemy. Although these symbols are not commonly used in scientific fields today, and it's unlikely that you'll encounter them, they may still be found in some texts. For instance, the symbol ⊙ may be used when discussing hydrogen. Iron is listed as □ in some documents.

Alchemical symbols are sometimes used for elements. The traditional male and female symbols of ♂ and ♀ are often used to respectively refer to iron and copper, for instance.

Chapter 11 – Science: Physics

Physics is an aspect of science that deals with matter and how it moves through space and time. Force and energy are also included in the study of physics, as are waves, movements and other actions that are experienced or felt.

General Motion

Motion occurs when an item departs from its state of rest. When one object is compared with another, a frame of reference is required. This includes an object in motion at a rate that can be compared with another object in the same setting.

Kinematics involves the study of the motion of objects irrespective of the forces that cause the motion. Various equations may be used when determining motion. The velocity of the general motion may be measured based on the change in the position of the object or x versus a change in time as measured by Δt.

Newton stated that there are three laws of motion:

1. An object that is in motion will stay in motion unless an outside force impacts or acts upon it; an object at rest will stay at rest unless something causes it to move.

For instance, a stone in a garden will stay in its same spot unless something touches it and causes it to move. Newton's first law of motion is also known as the law of inertia.

2. The force on an object will be equal to the object's mass multiplied by its acceleration.

Newton's second law of motion can be summarized as $f = ma$, where force is equal to the mass of something and a is acceleration. For instance, a fly that has a mass of 20 grams could be moving at a speed of 0.5 meters per second per second or m/s^2. If you use Newton's formula and multiply 20 (the fly's mass) by 0.5 (the fly's acceleration), you'll find the fly is moving at a force of 10 newtons. A Newton is a unit of force equal to the force required to cause a kilogram of mass to accelerate at one meter per second per second.

The general measurement of the Newton is variable based on an object's mass. The more newtons an object has, the harder it is to move.

3. There is always an equal and opposite reaction to every action.

Newton's third law of motion states that for every force there will always be an equal and opposite force or reaction. For instance, consider two vehicles that crash into each other. Regardless of the masses of those vehicles and how fast they were going, the force experienced by the vehicle that was hit is equal to and opposite to the force experienced by the other vehicle involved in the crash.

Acceleration

Acceleration, measured in m/s^2, is a measure of speed or velocity. Divide the velocity of an object by the time involved to find the general acceleration rate.

For instance, an object is moving at a velocity of 50 meters per second or m/s. This is occurring in 10 seconds of time. 50 divided by 10 is the rate of acceleration, which is 5 m/s^2.

You may also use this equation to determine the rate of deceleration. Subtract the final velocity from the initial velocity. This will produce a negative number. Then divide that number by the time to get the rate of deceleration. For example, if an object travels from 65 to 10 miles per hour in 5 seconds: $10 - 65 = -55$. Divide -55 by 5 to calculate a deceleration rate of -11 m/s^2.

The Difference Between Speed and Velocity

Speed is the distance covered in time. For example, how long it would take for you to travel a certain distance in a certain length of time. Speed does not necessarily take into account direction.

Velocity is the rate of change in motion of an object. This is the shortest distance between where an object started to move and its final destination.

Projectile Motion

Projectile motion is when an object is launched into the air, producing a parabolic motion. The item will rise in elevation as the object is thrown or launched. Provided there is no outside propulsion, the object will reach a maximum height (its apex) and then fall. The rate of the drop may be greater than the rate of ascent.

When the angle of launch is greater, the maximum height of a projectile will be higher. For instance, an item that is launched or thrown at a 60-degree angle from the ground will go higher than something thrown at a 40-degree angle. The range that the item will travel will be longer when the angle is lower. The 40-degree object will travel further from the launch point with regards to where it lands versus the 60-degree angle launch point.

All objects will experience the same rate of acceleration when heading toward the earth's surface. In accordance with the earth's gravitational pull, all objects will fall at a rate of $9.8 \, m/s^2$. The peak of an object's path will dictate when this gravitational pull starts to occur.

Friction

Friction is a force that challenges or impedes the motion of an object such as wind gusts or something an object is tethered to. You can produce a coefficient of friction by dividing the force of friction by the amount of force that would normally be experienced in a situation.

The force needed to move an object must be greater than the friction opposing the motion. The force needed to maintain the motion will be equal to the force of kinetic friction that encourages the movement.

In order to calculate the amount of friction, the mass of an object is multiplied by the rate of gravity, which is $9.8 \, m/s^2$. For instance, an object with a mass of 50 kg would have a friction of 490 newtons. You can also calculate static friction by dividing the regular frictional force by the normal force involved.

When it takes place in the air, friction is referred to as drag or air resistance. When it occurs in water, friction is referred to as viscosity.

Rotation

Rotation is when an object moves around its own axis. An example of this is a spinning top. The rotating motion can be consistent for a period of time provided there is enough force involved. Other natural forms of friction will have an influence on the movement of the spinning object.

The mass of an object will dictate the rate of rotation. The larger the mass, the greater the force required to make the object rotate. An object will rotate faster when the mass is more concentrated and closer to the center of the object.

Energy

An object needs energy to move and remain in motion.

Potential energy is a measure of the stored energy that an object has and includes energy due to the height of the object from the ground.

Kinetic energy occurs when something is in motion. For instance, a roller coaster on the top of a hill has potential energy when it is not moving. The roller coaster has kinetic energy when it gets past the top and moves downward quickly.

The potential and kinetic energy of an object are added together to find the total mechanical energy. While energy cannot be created or destroyed, it can be changed.

What Produces Kinetic Energy with a Mechanical Advantage?

A mechanical advantage is an outside force that assists kinetic energy or any other kind of energy with moving an object forward.

There are several types of mechanical advantages:

1. Inclined Plane – an object that will allow something to roll up or down a level

2. Wedge – something used to rotate an object

3. Pulley – an apparatus that helps lift a weight

4. Wheel and axle – a small vehicular apparatus that assists in propelling objects

5. Screw – a simple machine that is an inclined plane wrapped around a cylinder

6. Lever – an inclined plane with the fulcrum at the end of the lever that is placed under a weight to be lifted

Tides

The earth's gravitational pull is not the only force that acts upon objects. The pull of the moon directly influences the tides around the world. Tides change throughout the day as water levels start to change.

A tide is produced by the combined gravitational pulls of the moon and the earth's natural rotation. A tidal force develops from the gravitational pull of the moon.

A high tide develops when the gravitational pull of the moon pulls the water. The added tidal force produced by high tide cause the water to rise near shore. As the pull of the moon becomes less intense, the water starts to recede, producing a low tide.

As a result of the changes in the gravitational pull, there are two high tides and two low tides each day. The specific times of those tides will vary based on the time of the year and the positioning of the earth to the moon and sun.

Two Mechanical Waves

Mechanical waves go through various mediums, such as gas, liquid and solid materials.

1. Longitudinal

A longitudinal wave moves parallel to the direction a wave is traveling. The energy that arises through the wave will move along the distance of that wave and may dissipate after a certain length of time.

2. Transverse

A transverse wave moves perpendicular to the direction the wave is traveling. The wave will oscillate and form peaks and valleys.

Both longitudinal and transverse waves have energy, light and sound that is carried along a surface. Energy may also be conveyed within a vacuum depending on the quality of the waves.

Sound Impacts

Sounds can travel far in many directions. It's critical to understand many of the specific concepts pertaining to how sounds are conveyed and how to identify their locations and intensities.

The Doppler Effect occurs when sound quality changes based on your location to the object producing the sound. As an object moves in your direction, the sound waves appear shorter with more vibrations. An object that is far away or receding will produce waves that appear longer and slower.

Light Movement and Electromagnetic Waves

Light, which travels at 3.00×10^8 meters per second, moves as a wave front. A light is measured by its wavelength, which is the length for the light to complete a single cycle. However, not all light is visible. Light with a wavelength of 400 to 700 nm is visible, and this includes various colors. Red and orange are 700 nm, while blue and purple are closer to 400 nm.

The types of light include many types of electromagnetic waves that can directly influence the quality of what you can see. This listing of electromagnetic waves is based on their approximate wavelengths:

Radio waves – 30 mm and greater

Radio waves are light waves that carry signals that can be read by radio transmitters and decoders. Anything that emits heat radiation will also emit radio waves.

Microwaves – 1-30 mm

Microwaves are smaller and can move through smoke, clouds, rain and other obstructions that might interfere with radio waves. A microwave carries radar reports and computer data transmissions on landlines. Microwaves can also produce heat.

Infrared – 700 nm to 1 mm

Infrared waves are invisible heat waves. Radiation produced by fire and other heat-producing items will emit infrared waves. Some short-range infrared signals that do not produce heat are used in remote controls and imaging machines.

Ultraviolet – 10 to 400 nm

The wavelengths of ultraviolet light are shorter than visible light waves. High temperatures influence the quality of the heat produced. Ultraviolet rays can be powerful and can potentially harm your skin if you are exposed to them for a long period of time.

X-rays – 0.01 to 10 nm

X-rays, created by intense forms of heat, produce high amounts of energy. Black holes emit particularly large x-ray totals. X-rays are used for imaging. They are extremely dangerous if a subject is exposed to them for too long without protection.

Gamma rays – under 0.01 nm

Gamma rays are dangerous high-frequency waves emitted by black holes and neutron stars. These rays move through the empty spaces in an atom. Gamma rays can destroy cells if the body is not protected, especially during medical imaging. The earth's atmosphere can absorb gamma rays.

Chapter 12 – The Use of Numbers

The following chapter is an extension of the science portion of the AFOQT exam and includes working with many standards you will use in your regular duties in the Air Force.

Scientific Notations

Scientific notations are numbers that indicate multiples. For example, 5,000,000 may be written as 5×10^6. The number '6' is the exponent of 10. This means that 10 is multiplied by itself six times (10 x10x10x10x10x10).

You might be asked to simplify 1,250,000,000. If you move the decimal point nine places to the right to get 1.25, the nine places is represented by 10^9. The simplified expression is 1.25×10^9.

For decimal points, you would have to use a negative exponent. For example, the number .0000045 can be simplified by moving the decimal point six places to the right and multiplying it by 10 with an exponent of -6, which is expressed as 4.5×10^{-6}.

Temperature

Temperature is measured by three different systems:

1. Fahrenheit

Fahrenheit is the temperature scale used in the United States. Fahrenheit is based on 32 degrees as the freezing point of water and 212 degrees as the boiling point. The human body temperature is an average of 98.6 degrees Fahrenheit.

2. Celsius

Most of the world uses the Celsius scale for temperatures and it is the standard used in most sciences. This is also known as centigrade, as the Celsius measurement system is based on 100 parts. The freezing point of water is 0 degrees and 100 degrees is the boiling point of water. The average human body temperature is 37 degrees Celsius.

3. Kelvin

The Kelvin system is based on thermodynamics. The system is used in science. The freezing point of water in the Kelvin system is 273.15 kelvins. Absolute zero, the coldest possible temperature, is reached when something measures 0 kelvins.

To convert one standard to another, use the following formulas as appropriate:

Celsius to Fahrenheit: 9/5(Celsius) + 32

Fahrenheit to Celsius: 5/9(Fahrenheit – 32)

Celsius to Kelvin: C + 273.15

Note that there is no direct way to convert Kelvin to Fahrenheit or vice versa. In order to do so, the Celsius standard has to be used.

The Metric System

The metric system, or International System of Units, is used in every country in the world with the exception of the United States, Liberia and Burma (Myanmar).

Prefixes of the Metric System

Multiples

Prefix	Number	Symbol
Deca	10 (10^1)	Da
Hecto	100 (10^2)	H
Kilo	1,000 (10^3)	K
Mega	10^6	M
Giga	10^9	G
Tera	10^{12}	T
Peta	10^{15}	P
Exa	10^{18}	E

Submultiples

Prefix	Number	Symbol

Deci	0.1 (10^{-1})	D
Centi	0.01 (10^{-2})	C
Milli	0.001 (10^{-3})	M
Micro	10^{-6}	μ
Nano	10^{-9}	N
Pico	10^{-12}	P
Femto	10^{-15}	F
Atto	10^{-18}	A

Standards In the Metric System

1. Length

Length is measured in meters (m). Meters may be divided into centimeters or cm (100 cm = 1 m) or millimeters or mm (1000 mm = 1 m, or 10 mm = 1 cm).

To convert inches to centimeters: 1 inch = 2.54 cm (12 inches = 2.54 x 12 = 30.48 cm)

To convert miles to kilometers: 1 mile = 0.6214 km (100 miles = 0.6214 ÷ 100 = 62.14 km)

To convert kilometers to miles: 1 km = 0.6214 miles (100 km = 100 x 0.6214 = 62.14 miles)

2. Area

Area is a measurement expressed in square units. To find the number of square feet in a square use the following formula: s x s or s^2; to find the area of a rectangle, use l x w. For instance, a rectangle with a length measuring 15 cm and a width of 20 cm will have an area of 15 x 20 = 300 square centimeters.

3. Volume

The volume of an object is calculated in cubic units:

Volume of a cube = s³ (s x s x s) A cube whose sides each measure 5 cm will have a volume of 5³ = 5x5x5 = 125 cubic centimeters.

Volume rectangular brick = l x w x h. For example, an object with sides that measure 5, 8 and 10 meters is calculated by l x w x h = 5 x 8 x 10 = 400 cubic meters.

4. Weight

Weight is measured in grams and kilograms and not pounds. One kilogram (kg) is equal to 2.2 pounds.

To convert pounds to kilograms: 1 pound = 0.45592 kg. (100 lbs. = 100 x 0.45592 = 45.593 kg.)

5. Liquid Mass

Liquid masses can be measured based on liters and not quarts or gallons.

To convert gallons to liters: 1 gallon = 3.785 liters (40 gallons = 40 x 3.785 = 151.4 liters).

To convert liters to gallons: liters ÷ 3.785 = gallons.

6. Time

Time measurement is the same for traditional systems and the metric system, the same second, hour, and day. However, military time is based on the 24-hour clock. Noon is 1200 hours; midnight is 2400 hours. For instance, 4:50 PM would be 1650 hours; 1:00 AM is 0100 hours.

7. Speed

While traditional speed measurements are miles or kilometers per hour, another measurement is meters per second or m/s.

8. Acceleration

Acceleration is a measure of the change of speed. For instance, a person may go from 4 m/s to 6 m/s when running. This would be measured as an acceleration rate of two meters per second per second. This is written as m/s^2.

9. Force

Force is a measurement of how much force it takes for one kilogram of weight to move at an acceleration rate of 1 m/s^2. The measurement used is called a newton. For instance, working at 30 newtons means that it would take 30 kg m/s^2 to move forward.

Power Sources

This segment will focus on many of the power sources that you might encounter when dealing with engines and other power-related machines.

1. Watts

A watt is a unit of power using the International System of Units as a rate of energy transfer. A watt is the rate of work used to power something. One watt is equal to one ampere with the voltage of one volt. A machine with more watts produces more power. When wattage is higher, energy is greater.

Some radio stations operate on 50 kilowatts or kW of power. For instance, WLW-AM in Cincinnati uses a transmitter that operates at 50 kW of power. The added power allows the station to be heard well beyond the city of Cincinnati depending on weather conditions and the interference of other radio signals.

2. Amperes

An ampere (also referred to as an amp) is a unit of electric current based on the ratio of charge flowing through a conductor. An ampere measures the current generated by one volt moving through the resistance of one ohm. Some ampere flows may be dangerous.

223

3. Volts

A volt is a scientific unit for electrical force. The volt is the difference of potential that can drive an ampere of current against one ohm of resistance. Voltage is the pressure at which energy is produced. A unit with more voltage has more energy. An AA, AAA, C or D battery operates on 1.5 volts or V of power. A 9V battery works on 9 volts, hence the name. Anything with a high voltage can cause an electrical shock and may be deadly.

4. Ohms

An ohm is the amount of electrical resistance that restricts the flow of an electrical current. The ohm may be represented by the Greek letter omega or Ω.

5. Horsepower

Horsepower or hp refers to the power needed to raise 550 pounds a distance of one foot in one second. This is also the power needed to move 33,000 pounds by one foot in one minute. These numbers are based on the British Imperial System. According to the International System of Units, one hp is 746 watts of power.

6. BTU

A British Thermal Unit or BTU is a unit of heat. The BTU measurement is the amount of heat necessary to raise the temperature of water by one degree Fahrenheit. More BTUs are needed to heat a large area or volume.

Science Questions

1. The atomic number of an element is based on:
   a. Protons
   b. Neutrons
   c. Electrons
   d. Atomic mass
   e. All of the above

2. What makes an isotope distinct?
   a. It dictates the electrons
   b. A different number of neutrons are included in each isotope
   c. Every isotope has a varying number of protons
   d. Isotopes come in different weights
   e. No real difference

3. What type of chemical reaction is critical for the operation of a jet engine?
   a. Combination
   b. Decomposition
   c. Combustion
   d. Oxidation
   e. Any of these can work

4. How many carbon atoms are found in $C_3H_6O_4$?
   a. 3
   b. 4
   c. 6
   d. 9
   e. 13

5. Which pH level is associated with something that is the most acidic?
   a. 2.4
   b. 5.5
   c. 7.5
   d. 11.3
   e. 13.1

6. Which pH level is the closest to neutral?
    a. 4.5
    b. 6.8
    c. 8.4
    d. 10.3
    e. 11.3

7. What form of decay occurs when an atom emits 2 protons and 2 neutrons from its nucleus?
    a. Alpha
    b. Beta
    c. Gamma
    d. Theta
    e. None of the above

8. What can be noticed in an isotope to determine how unstable it is?
    a. Atomic number
    b. Atomic mass
    c. Variability of atoms
    d. Number of protons
    e. Number of electrons

9. What element can be found at the beginning of the expression for an acid?
    a. Oxygen
    b. Nitrogen
    c. Helium
    d. Carbon
    e. Hydrogen

10. What element is at the end of an expression for a base element?
    a. Water
    b. Helium
    c. Carbon monoxide
    d. Hydroxide
    e. Carbon trioxide

11. 2 H_2O is a combination that is:
    a. Two parts of H_2O
    b. H_4O_2
    c. H_2O with 2 parts
    d. Two separate elements
    e. A division between hydrogen and oxygen

12. What can be used as a measurement of mass?
    a. Kilogram
    b. Ampere
    c. Meter
    d. Kilometer
    e. Second

13. Energy that originates from the planet's internal heat source is known as:
    a. Geothermal
    b. Volcanic
    c. Solar
    d. Hydroelectric
    e. Thermodynamic

14. What type of element is more likely to go through alpha decay?
    a. Something with a larger atomic number
    b. A lightweight element
    c. A thick compound
    d. Most types of gases
    e. All of the above

15. What can be used to block gamma radiation?
    a. Paper
    b. Wood
    c. Aluminum
    d. Steel
    e. Lead

16. You would require more BTU if:
    a. An engine is very large
    b. An engine has to go faster
    c. You have more power to work with
    d. You need to keep the voltage on something done
    e. You have a larger area of surface to work with

17. When an engine has more horsepower, that means the engine can:
    a. Go faster
    b. Accelerate well
    c. Keep from overheating
    d. Produce enough heat
    e. Handle more weight

18. The voltage on an object is necessary for:
    a. Keeping the heat on something under control
    b. Grounding a source
    c. Helping to distribute power
    d. Allowing for a charge
    e. Getting more energy ready

19. How is 1,500,000 expressed as a scientific notation?
    a. 1.5×10^5
    b. 1.5×10^6
    c. 15×10^5
    d. 1.5×10^4
    e. 1.5×10^7

20. How is 0.00054 expressed as a scientific notation?
    a. 5.4×10^4
    b. 0.054×10^4
    c. 5.4×10^{-4}
    d. 0.54×10^{-4}
    e. 54×10^{-4}

21. What is 110 degrees Fahrenheit in Celsius?
    a. 42.5
    b. 43.3
    c. 45
    d. 45.5
    e. 46.3

22. What is -15 degrees Celsius in Fahrenheit?
    a. 5
    b. -5
    c. 4
    d. 9
    e. -9

23. What is 45 degrees Celsius in Kelvins?
    a. 95.15
    b. 250.15
    c. 305.15
    d. 318.15
    e. 343.15

24. How many gigabytes on a computer hard drive are in one terabyte?
    a. 0.1
    b. 100
    c. 1,000
    d. 1,000,000
    e. 1,000,000,000

25. One nanogram is equal to how many grams?
    a. 0.00001
    b. 0.000001
    c. 0.0000001
    d. 0.00000001
    e. 0.000000001

26. Which of these distances is the longest?
    a. 1.5 miles
    b. 3 kilometers
    c. 2,600 meters
    d. 3,000 feet
    e. 1,000 yards

27. How many liters of fuel is 15 gallons?
    a. 41.25
    b. 46.87
    c. 56.78
    d. 60
    e. 65

28. Tides are produced by:
    a. Temperature changes
    b. The gravitational pull between the earth and moon
    c. The gravitational pull between the earth and sun
    d. Amount of light
    e. Elevation changes

29. When you multiply the mass of an object by its velocity, you will determine the object's:
    a. Force
    b. Acceleration rate
    c. Speed
    d. Effort
    e. Momentum

30. Which of the following can be used as a simple machine to produce a mechanical advantage?
    a. Wedge
    b. Pulley
    c. Lever
    d. Screw
    e. All of the above

31. This element has the smallest atomic mass:
    a. Hydrogen
    b. Helium
    c. Lithium
    d. Beryllium
    e. Boron

32. Kinetic energy only occurs when something is:
    a. At rest
    b. High above the ground
    c. On the ground level
    d. Stopping
    e. Moving

33. An object rests on a surface. Gravity is impacting its mass. What is this referred to as?
    a. Weight
    b. Size
    c. Pressure
    d. Elevation
    e. Friction

34. If you were to throw a ball into the air, the ball would reach the greatest height if you were to throw that ball at what angle?
    a. 30
    b. 45
    c. 60
    d. 75
    e. 80

35. Velocity is different from speed in that velocity is:
    a. Speed based on movement
    b. Speed based on the positions changed
    c. Shifts around the places that you travel
    d. Speed based on moving on a straight line
    e. Lift changes

36. Which element has a symbol that does not have letters in its name?
    a. Fluorine
    b. Aluminum
    c. Mercury
    d. Sulfur
    e. Zirconium

37. How much acceleration would an object have if its velocity was constant?
    a. At least 10 m/s^2
    b. At least 100 m/s^2
    c. Nothing
    d. The item may go in reverse
    e. Varies by mass

38. Can an object that is in motion keep on going in motion?
    a. At all times
    b. Until an outside force gets in the way
    c. Depends on weight
    d. If there is enough of an incline or decline
    e. Any of these can work

39. What can you notice when you see an atomic number 5 on an element of 5 versus an atomic number of 14?
    a. The second element has a greater mass
    b. The second element has more protons
    c. The first element has a longer half-life
    d. The first element has more protons
    e. A and B

40. A periodic table lists Copper with the following details: 29, Cu, 63.546. What can be said about the number 29?
    a. It is the atomic number
    b. It is the atomic mass
    c. It is the isotope of that element that you are more likely to experience in nature
    d. It is the number of isotopes you could find surrounding the element
    e. None of the above

41. Which of these elements is a liquid?
    a. Cadmium
    b. Bismuth
    c. Iodine
    d. Mercury
    e. Arsenic

42. Which of these elements is an alkali metal?
    a. Magnesium
    b. Sodium
    c. Yttrium
    d. Zirconium
    e. Titanium

43. Where on the periodic table are the noble gases located?
    a. On the right-most column
    b. In the middle part of the table
    c. On the second-left column
    d. On the top row
    e. They are scattered all around the table

44. The periodic table for antimony features the following: 51, Sb, 121.76. Which of the following is incorrect?
    a. 51 is the number of electrons in the element
    b. Sb is the symbol for antimony
    c. 121.76 is the atomic mass of the element
    d. 51 is the atomic number of the element
    e. All of the above

45. Which of these is a base?
    a. HCl
    b. RbOH
    c. HNO_3
    d. CO_2
    e. LiPo

46. What makes an uncatalyzed pathway distinct?
    a. It is hard to figure out where the energy on a reaction would go
    b. A reactant would produce a delayed result
    c. The surface area for the response of something would be small in size
    d. The energy on a reaction is more predictable
    e. None of the above

47. Decomposition occurs when an element:
    a. Is broken down into a few additional products
    b. Links to produce one larger compound
    c. Loses enough of its properties so that it produces only one element
    d. Loses its oxygen stores
    e. Gains extra oxygen

48. As Bohr's model for an atom is described, an electron would appear on the:
    a. Nucleus
    b. Energy level
    c. Orbit
    d. Proton layout
    e. None of the above

49. A hectogram is how many times the base value of a gram?
    a. 10
    b. 100
    c. 1,000
    d. 1/10
    e. 1/100

50. How would you write 9×10^5 if it is written in its full form?
     a. 90,000
     b. 900,000
     c. 9,000,000
     d. 90,000,000
     e. 0.9

51. 10^{-3} is equal to:
     a. 0.001
     b. 0.0001
     c. 0.00001
     d. 0.01
     e. 0.1

52. The Bel scale measures the intensity of:
     a. Vibrations
     b. Speed
     c. Gravity
     d. Sound
     e. Weight

53. A metalloid is:
     a. Mostly a nonmetal material
     b. Material with a shiny surface
     c. An element with a mix of metal and nonmetal properties
     d. A surface that is very rough
     e. An material that is highly malleable

54. The Doppler effect states that when you move toward something that is making noise, the sound:
     a. Does not produce much noise
     b. Becomes less distinct
     c. Blends in with other noises
     d. Dissipates
     e. Becomes more intense

55. The frequency of the sound waves in the Doppler effect is dictated by:
     a. Size
     b. Volume
     c. Speed
     d. Distance
     e. Position

56. How is radium produced?
    a. Heating
    b. Freezing
    c. Decay
    d. Melding
    e. Radiation

57. What element is listed under the symbol C?
    a. Chlorine
    b. Calcium
    c. Cobalt
    d. Copper
    e. Carbon

58. Redshift occurs on the Doppler effect when the waves:
    a. Are longer
    b. Are shorter
    c. Are taller
    d. Are slimmer
    e. May occur at any time

59. Interference occurs within a wave when something:
    a. Amplifies the wave
    b. Impacts the wave
    c. Keeps the wave from working
    d. Gets in the natural movement of the wave
    e. Causes the wave to stop working and then go back to working at random

60. What can an electric current do to manage magnetic forces?
    a. Reflect items
    b. Control the flow of energy
    c. Reduce the power of a surface
    d. Deflect items
    e. Generate energy

61. What reactions entail the breaking and reproduction of bonds between atoms?
    a. Nuclear
    b. Electron
    c. Physical
    d. Chemical
    e. Isotonic

62. An object is traveling from 20 m/s to 40 m/s in 20 seconds. What is the rate of acceleration?
    a. 1 m/s^2
    b. 1 m/s
    c. 10 m/s
    d. 10 m/s^2
    e. 2 m/s

63. A vast majority of the mass inside an atom is found in the:
    a. Electrons
    b. Protons
    c. Nucleus
    d. Neutrons
    e. Orbit patterns

64. What makes an isotope different from another in an atom?
    a. Neutron total
    b. Electron number
    c. Proton number
    d. Nucleus density
    e. Orbit patterns laid out

65. If 2 items were to combine to produce a reactant, what type of action happens?
    a. Collaboration of enzymes
    b. Combustion
    c. Decomposition
    d. Combination
    e. Oxidation

66. How does a catalyst impact the rate of a reaction?
    a. Reactants are kept down in density
    b. The temperature within a reaction is kept in check
    c. The concentration of reactants will increase, thus producing added reactions
    d. The products that are produced in the reaction will be minimal
    e. The activation energy needed for the process to work will be minimal

67. How are the elements in a single column similar to one another on the periodic table?
    a. Density is the same
    b. Atomic number is the same
    c. The chemical properties are similar
    d. The electrons are arranged in the same way
    e. Nothing very distinct

68. Kinematics is a study of:
    a. Mass
    b. Force
    c. Time
    d. Movement
    e. Positioning

69. The law of inertia, according to Newton, states the following:
    a. There is always an equal and opposite reaction for every action that takes place.
    b. The velocity of an object is equal to the change in its position divided by the time.
    c. A force that acts upon an object is equal to the mass multiplied by the acceleration.
    d. An object that is at rest will stay at rest unless an outside force impacts it. The object will also stay in motion until an outside force impedes it.
    e. The momentum of the object is based on the mass and velocity of the object in motion.

70. What can be said about actinoids?
    a. They are radioactive
    b. They appear in the 90 range in terms of atomic numbers
    c. These man-made
    d. Such items can be risky if handled improperly
    e. All of the above

71. What can be said about a noble gas?
    a. It is radioactive
    b. You can notice it in the air
    c. There is a distinct odor to each noble gas
    d. It does not react much to chemicals
    e. All of the above

72. Which of the follow elements is a liquid?
    a. Bromine
    b. Iodine
    c. Fluorine
    d. Sulfur
    e. Boron

73. What can be said about the element Gold?
    a. It is fragile
    b. Added reactions may be produced in its sub-shell
    c. The compound can potentially be melted down
    d. A and B
    e. All of the above

74. Which pH number is the most neutral?
    a. 5.5
    b. 6.5
    c. 7.8
    d. 8.3
    e. 9.0

75. When an electron leaves the neutron of an atom, what form of decay occurs?
    a. Alpha
    b. Beta
    c. Gamma
    d. Theta
    e. Unclear

76. UI is an isotope of:
    a. Radon
    b. Tritium
    c. Uranium
    d. Thorium
    e. Protactinium

77. The decay chain of uranium can produce what particular element?
    a. Radium
    b. Polonium
    c. Bismuth
    d. Lead
    e. Thorium

78. Thorium can decay into what element?
    a. Thallium
    b. Polonium
    c. Bismuth
    d. Lead
    e. All of the above

79. Actinium can decay into what element?
    a. Bismuth
    b. Uranium
    c. Radon
    d. Curium
    e. Radium

80. What is the greatest concern about actinium?
    a. Unpredictable decay
    b. Highly radioactive
    c. Heavy weight
    d. Not many isotopes are stable
    e. All of the above

81. ^{212}Pb is an isotope of:
    a. Lead
    b. Polonium
    c. Bismuth
    d. Thallium
    e. Radon

82. The compounds inside a battery are:
    a. Alkaline
    b. Acidic
    c. Neutral
    d. Depends on the charge
    e. No identifiable pH changes

83. Ammonia is a material that is:
    a. Alkaline
    b. Acidic
    c. Neutral
    d. Depends on its composure
    e. No identifiable pH charges

84. What pH level is appropriate for tap water?
    a. 4
    b. 5
    c. 6
    d. 7
    e. 8

85. What would happen to the pH of water if it were to be carbonated?
    a. Become more acidic
    b. Become more alkaline
    c. Move toward neutrality
    d. No distinguishable change
    e. Varies by quantity

86. What can be said about sugary foods?
    a. They have low pH totals
    b. Their pH levels are neutral
    c. They have high pH totals
    d. These may vary by quantity
    e. Sugar and other items could influence how something works

87. Isotopes are often associated with:
    a. Mutations
    b. Alterations
    c. Radiation
    d. Melting
    e. Heat

88. What makes an unknown gas on the periodic table distinct?
    a. It is inert
    b. It produces a scent or color
    c. It comes from many isotopes
    d. The gas is radioactive
    e. The stability is unclear

89. Are alchemical symbols necessary in chemistry?
    a. Depends on the situation
    b. They could be used, but they are not needed
    c. They are heavily outdated
    d. May work in all situations
    e. No clear solution

90. Is there is a limit to how many elements may appear on the periodic table?
    a. Yes, up to 130
    b. Yes, up to 150
    c. Yes, the table cannot be changed any further
    d. No real limit
    e. Depends on the types of elements

91. What rays operate with the lowest wavelength?
    a. Gamma rays
    b. X-rays
    c. Infrared
    d. Microwave
    e. Radio waves

92. What color of visible light has the lowest wavelength?
    a. Red
    b. Yellow
    c. Green
    d. Blue
    e. Purple

93. X-rays are used for:
    a. Screening inside the body
    b. Heating foods
    c. Drying items
    d. Transmitting radio information
    e. All of the above

94. Which type of electromagnetic wave is likely to be interfered with the most?
   a. Radio waves
   b. Microwaves
   c. Infrared waves
   d. Visible light waves
   e. Ultraviolet light

95. What makes ultraviolet waves dangerous?
   a. They can cause cancer
   b. They can cause sunburns
   c. They are extremely bright
   d. They may wear you out physically
   e. A and B

96. What happens when the wavelength of a light becomes smaller?
   a. The light is increasingly visible
   b. The light is easy to interfere with
   c. The light is dark in tone
   d. You can heat things with the light
   e. The light becomes more dangerous

97. Radio waves are received by:
   a. Television sets
   b. Radio receivers
   c. Computers
   d. Radio towers
   e. All of the above

98. A landline phone system uses what waves?
   a. Radio waves
   b. Microwaves
   c. Infrared waves
   d. Ultraviolet waves
   e. X-rays

99. What is the wavelength of Red visible light?
   a. 400
   b. 450
   c. 500
   d. 600
   e. 700

100.   Gamma rays are known for having more:
   a. Stability
   b. Functionality
   c. Energy
   d. Heat
   e. Use

Science Answers

1. a. The atomic number refers to the number of protons in an element.
2. b. Each isotope has the same number of protons, but the neutrons will vary.
3. c. Combustion is critical for ensuring that fuel can break down and produce the gas needed for allowing the engine to work as it should.
4. a. The subscript next to the element number refers to the number of atoms in that element. The subscript here shows that there are 3 carbon atoms in the combination.
5. a. A lower pH number means that something is more acidic. 2.4 is the lowest number in this list, thus the item is highly acidic.
6. b. A neutral pH is 7.
7. a. Alpha decay is found in heavy atoms that have more of these protons and neutrons to shed.
8. b. The atomic mass can show how different the isotope is. A and D are both the same thing and are incorrect.
9. e. An acid element combination always appears with hydrogen or H at the beginning of the expression.
10. d. Hydroxide or OH indicates a base element. This should appear at the end of the expression.
11. a. When there is a number at the beginning of an expression for an element, this means that the element has 2 parts of that particular element in the combination.
12. a. The kilogram is used to designate mass and 1,000 grams equals one kilogram or kg.
13. e. Geothermal energy occurs comes from deep within the earth's core where the temperature is intensely hot.

14. a. Alpha radiation can be found in many larger elements that have more weight.
15. e. Gamma radiation can only be blocked by lead.
16. e. The BTUs are used when heating a space. You would require more BTUs to heat a large area than what would be needed for a small area.
17. e. Horsepower is required for allowing something heavy to be moved. The greater the weight, the greater the horsepower needed.
18. c. More volts mean more power.
19. b. You would move the decimal point 6 places to the left.
20. c. The exponent for the scientific notation is negative when considering a decimal number. Move the decimal point 4 places to the right.
21. b. Subtract 110 -32 = 78, and then multiply 78 x 5/9 = 43.3.
22. a. Multiply -15 x 9/5 = -27, and then add 32 = 5 degrees Fahrenheit.
23. d. Add 273.15 + 45 to determine the number of Kelvins in the equation.
24. c. Giga is a prefix for 10^9, and tera is a prefix for 10^{12}. One terabyte would equal 1,000 gigabytes.
25. e. Nano is a prefix for 10^{-9}. E is the correct answer.
26. b. D and E are both of the same length. 2,600 meters is 2.6 kilometers, which would rule out C. 3 kilometers is equal to about 1.86 miles, thus making B the correct answer.
27. c. To convert gallons to liters: gallons x 3.785.
28. b. The gravitational pull causes waves in the oceans.
29. e. The momentum is the mass of an object multiplied by its velocity.
30. e. In addition to these 4 items, an inclined plane or a wheel and axle may be used to produce a mechanical advantage.
31. a. The 5 elements listed here are all the 5 lightest elements based on atomic mass. However, hydrogen is the lightest with an atomic weight of 1.008.

32. e. Kinetic energy occurs when an object is in motion.

33. a. Weight is impacted by how easily the object can be moved.

34. e. When you throw something at a greater angle, the item will move higher in the air, but it will also travel the shortest distance. This is provided that the same amount of force is used when launching the object.

35. b. The positions that you would travel will make a greater impact based on what is in an area.

36. c. Mercury has the symbol Hg, which comes from the Latin name for the compound, hydrargyrum.

37. c. When the velocity is constant, there is no change in the rate of travel. Therefore, the acceleration rate would be zero.

38. b. The first of Newton's laws of motion states that an object in motion will stay in motion until the object is impacted.

39. e. When an element has a higher atomic number, it means it has a greater mass and more protons. The mass of an element with a higher number is always larger. The number of protons in the element will dictate its atomic number, and more protons will equal a greater atomic number.

40. a. The first number of an element on a periodic table is the atomic number. For copper, which is listed as Cu, the atomic number is 29.

41. d. Although many of these elements could potentially be melted to a liquid form, mercury is the only item that is specifically listed as a liquid.

42. b. The alkali metals on the periodic table are on the first column on the left on the periodic table. Sodium, lithium, potassium, and rubidium are among the alkali metals listed.

43. a. Helium, neon, xenon, and other noble gases appear on the far right of the periodic table.

44. a. The atomic number is the number of protons in the element, not the electrons.

45. b. A base can be identified by the OH at the end of the expression. Rubidium hydroxide, or RbOH, is the only base listed on this chart.

46. d. In an uncatalyzed pathway the energy will move up and down with a consistent flow. A catalyzed pathway would be difficult to predict.

47. a. Decomposition happens when a single element or reactant is broken down into 2 separate items.

48. b. The energy levels that orbit around the nucleus are where the electrons are found.

49. b. A hectogram is equal to 100 grams. A kilogram is equal to 1,000 grams, and a decigram is 0.1 grams.

50. b. The decimal is moved 5 places to the right.

51. a. The decimal point would move 3 places to the left from 1 as the exponent is negative.

52. d. The Bel scale indicates the loudness of the sound based on a certain value.

53. c. A metalloid is between a metal and nonmetal and expresses qualities of both parts.

54. e. The Doppler Effect states that the frequency and intensity of sound becomes more substantial when you are closer to the object that is producing the sound. The opposite occurs when the sound-making object is farther away; the sound decreases.

55. d. Distance is the most important factor regarding the Doppler Effect. The intensity and frequency of the sound waves becomes greater when you are closer to the object emitting the sound.

56. c. Radium is produced by the decay of uranium or thorium.

57. e. Chlorine, calcium, cobalt, and copper are listed by the symbols Cl, Ca, Co, and Cu respectively. Carbon is the element that uses the symbol C.

58. a. When the waves are longer, the sound produced is not as intense as you are further away from the object making the sound. The waves will produce a redshift pattern. The blueshift occurs when the waves are shorter in length and the object making the sound is approaching or is closer.

59. d. Any physical or audible object could get in the way of the wave and interfere, thus keeping the wave from being as effective.

60. e. You can generate energy through an electric current. The magnetic forces will become more significant or prominent in quality.

61. d. A chemical reaction happens when atoms switch between different substances.

62. a. The rate is based on meters per second per second. The object is rising by 1 m/s every second during that time period.

63. c. The nucleus features the neutrons and protons in the atom and make up almost all of the mass of the element.

64. a. When there are a different number of neutrons but the same number of protons, the atom is of a certain isotope.

65. d. The combination process involves 2 elements that mix in together to produce a reaction. The quality of the reaction will be based on the materials being mixed.

66. e. The activation energy will be lowered to facilitate the appropriate change that is to take place with a material.

67. c. The items in each column include different physical qualities, although they are all the same in each column. This includes a separate column for gases and another for metalloids.

68. d. The movement or motion of an object is the focus of kinematics.

69. d. Inertia is needed to keep objects active.

70. e. Actinoids are items that are based on actinium and can be harmful if they are not managed properly.

71. d. A noble gas will not often react to chemicals. Nobel gases have no color and no odor.

72. a. Bromine and mercury are the only 2 elements on the periodic table that are liquids.

73. e. As a transition metal, Gold is a fragile metal that can be melted down by heat.

74. b. The pH level of 7 is neutral. 6.5 is the closest choice to neutral.

75. b. Beta decay involves a new element being produced due to an electron leaving the neutron. The electron count will increase and will have a greater amount of radiation than alpha decay, although the radiation is not as dangerous or difficult to control as what is found in gamma decay.

76. c. UI is the symbol for Uranium I, which is a name for the ^{238}U isotope of uranium.

77. e. Thorium is directly produced, which in turn can decay into the other elements listed.

78. e. The decay chain covers all of these elements, although the specific element will vary by isotope.

79. a. The other elements in this question are too strong in the decay chain.

80. e. Actinium has many distinct isotopes that are hard to predict.

81. a. Pb is the chemical symbol of lead.

82. b. A battery contains acidic elements that can influence its functionality.

83. a. There are no acids in ammonia, although the compound itself can be dangerous if handled improperly.

84. d. Water is as neutral as possible.

85. a. Carbonation is similar to an acidic soft drink.

86. a. Sugars, particularly chocolates, are often acidic and therefore have low pH totals.

87. c. Radiation can impact isotopes in that different isotopes will decay into particular elements, especially when the elements are highly radioactive.

88. e. Further studies are required when looking at such gases to determine how functional they are and what to expect as they develop.

89. b. Alchemical symbols are not inaccurate, but they are archaic and difficult to use.

90. d. The periodic table has room for many elements that may be discovered in the future, and there are no limitations.

91. a. Gamma rays operate at under 0.01 nm.

92. e. Purple or violet light features an average wavelength of 400 nm.

93. a. X-rays are often used for diagnostic purposes.

94. a. Radio waves can be influenced by wind, water, and clouds among other natural obstructions that may cause interference.

95. e. Ultraviolet waves are known to cause sunburns and can cause cancer.

96. e. The light is dangerous because the materials may be unstable.

97. e. Radio waves are designed to carry and convey more data and should be easy to read by different materials.

98. b. The microwaves on a landline are designed to handle narrow channels versus what radio waves can manage.

99. e. The brighter red light would have the highest wavelength of all types of visible light.

100. c. When the light becomes more intense, the energy produced is more significant.

Chapter 13 – Reading Tables

There are many tables that you will be required to read in the Air Force. Such tables can include an immense amount of numbers and information.

The table-reading section of the AFOQT exam tests your ability to use the material presented in tables, including using coordinates on a chart.

Charts

In some cases, you will have to work with large information charts. You might be presented with geographic information, items used in an airport or details on what equipment is being used at a specific time. The information is plotted using a series of rows and columns.

The AFOQT exam may test you on your ability to find errors in such charts, as such errors can be significant.

Detailed Tables

Many of the tables in the AFOQT exam feature a series of numbers arranged based on their labeled x and y values. The x values are listed on the horizontal rows and the y values appear vertically in a series of columns.

There will be several numerical values on the table, all associated with one x point and one y point each. Your goal is to identify what the specific number is at a certain point. The question will be labeled with the x value listed first and then the y value.

For instance, you might be asked to identify the number represented by (2, -1). Using these coordinates, you will be asked to identify the specific number that appears on this part of the table.

Each table will have 6 to 10 questions. You will have about 10 seconds to answer each question. There will be multiple tables and charts of various types.

Tips

1. Focus on one coordinate at a time.

2. Avoid thinking about the clock.

3. Always mark an answer for a question even if you have to guess.

4. Always be aware of the labeling on each axis. Confirm the data on the x and y axes before working on a table.

Questions on Reading Tables

Note: Each table in this test is specifically for specific questions.

The following table is to be used for Questions 1-7:

Y v X >	-3	-2	-1	0	1	2	3
3	25	26	28	30	31	32	33
2	26	28	30	32	33	34	35
1	27	29	31	33	35	36	37
0	29	30	32	34	36	37	38
-1	30	32	33	35	37	38	40
-2	31	33	34	36	38	39	41
-3	32	34	35	37	39	40	42

1. (-3, -2)
    a. 27
    b. 29
    c. 30
    d. 31
    e. 32

2. (-2, 0)
    a. 29
    b. 30
    c. 32
    d. 34
    e. 36

3. (-3, -3)
    a. 32
    b. 34
    c. 37
    d. 39
    e. 42

4. (0, 3)
    a. 34
    b. 32
    c. 30
    d. 28
    e. 31

5. (-2, -1)
    a. 32
    b. 30
    c. 28
    d. 31
    e. 35

6. (3, 1)
    a. 33
    b. 35
    c. 37
    d. 38
    e. 40

7. (1, 0)
    a. 32
    b. 34
    c. 36
    d. 37
    e. 38

The following table is to be used for Questions 8-14:

Y v X >	-3	-2	-1	0	1	2	3
3	22	23	25	27	28	29	30
2	23	25	27	29	30	31	32
1	24	26	28	30	32	33	34
0	26	27	29	31	33	34	35
-1	27	29	30	32	34	35	37
-2	28	30	31	33	35	36	38
-3	29	31	32	34	36	37	39

8. $(0, 3)$
   a. 25
   b. 27
   c. 29
   d. 31
   e. 33

9. $(3, 2)$
   a. 30
   b. 32
   c. 34
   d. 36
   e. 38

10. $(0, -2)$
   a. 30
   b. 31
   c. 32
   d. 33
   e. 34

11. $(-2, -2)$
   a. 36
   b. 31
   c. 25
   d. 30
   e. 31

12. (0, -3)
    a. 31
    b. 34
    c. 39
    d. 36
    e. 30

13. (3, 3)
    a. 22
    b. 29
    c. 39
    d. 30
    e. 34

14. (-2, -1)
    a. 27
    b. 30
    c. 35
    d. 31
    e. 29

The following chart is to be used for Questions 15-23:

Y v X >	-4	-3	-2	-1	0	1	2	3	3
-4	33	34	35	37	38	39	41	42	43
-3	35	37	38	40	42	44	45	46	47
-2	36	38	39	41	42	44	46	47	48
-1	37	38	41	42	43	45	47	49	50
0	39	40	42	43	44	46	48	50	51
1	41	42	44	45	47	49	50	51	52
2	42	44	45	47	48	50	51	52	53
3	44	45	47	48	49	51	52	53	54
4	45	47	48	50	51	52	53	55	56

15. (-3, 1)
    a. 39
    b. 42
    c. 44
    d. 45
    e. 47

16. (-2, -2)
    a. 32
    b. 35
    c. 37
    d. 38
    e. 39

17. (3, -3)
    a. 42
    b. 43
    c. 44
    d. 45
    e. 46

18. (0, 0)
    a. 42
    b. 43
    c. 44
    d. 45
    e. 46

19. (3, 0)
    a. 50
    b. 51
    c. 52
    d. 53
    e. 54

20. (3, 4)
    a. 54
    b. 55
    c. 56
    d. 57
    e. 58

21. (-3, 4)
    a. 45
    b. 46
    c. 47
    d. 48
    e. 49

22. (-2, -1)
    a. 37
    b. 38
    c. 39
    d. 40
    e. 41

23. (0, 2)
    a. 46
    b. 47
    c. 48
    d. 49
    e. 50

The following table is to be used for Questions 24-33:

Y v X >	-4	-3	-2	-1	0	1	2	3	4
4	31	32	34	35	37	39	40	42	43
3	30	31	33	34	35	37	38	40	41
2	29	30	31	33	34	36	38	39	40
1	28	29	30	32	34	35	36	37	38
0	27	28	30	31	32	34	35	36	37
-1	26	27	28	29	31	33	34	35	36
-2	24	25	27	28	30	31	33	34	35
-3	23	24	26	27	28	30	31	33	34
-4	22	23	24	26	27	28	30	32	33

24. (-4, -4)
    a. 22
    b. 23
    c. 24
    d. 25
    e. 26

257

25. (-2, 2)
   a. 27
   b. 28
   c. 29
   d. 30
   e. 31

26. (2, -2)
   a. 30
   b. 31
   c. 32
   d. 33
   e. 34

27. (0, 3)
   a. 33
   b. 34
   c. 35
   d. 36
   e. 37

28. (-2, 4)
   a. 31
   b. 32
   c. 33
   d. 34
   e. 35

29. (-4, 2)
   a. 27
   b. 28
   c. 29
   d. 30
   e. 31

30. (-2, 0)
   a. 27
   b. 28
   c. 29
   d. 30
   e. 31

31. (3, 3)
   a. 37
   b. 38
   c. 39
   d. 40
   e. 41

32. (4, -1)
   a. 32
   b. 33
   c. 34
   d. 35
   e. 36

33. (2, 3)
   a. 35
   b. 36
   c. 37
   d. 38
   e. 39

The following table is to be used for Questions 34-43:

Y v X >	-3	-2	-1	0	1	2	3
3	25	26	27	28	29	30	31
2	28	29	30	31	32	33	34
1	45	46	47	48	49	50	51
0	15	16	17	18	19	20	21
-1	28	29	30	31	32	33	34
-2	31	32	33	34	35	36	37
-3	8	9	10	11	12	13	14

34. (3, 3)
   a. 30
   b. 31
   c. 32
   d. 33
   e. 34

35. (0, 3)
   a. 24
   b. 25
   c. 26
   d. 27
   e. 28

36. (-1, -2)
   a. 31
   b. 32
   c. 33
   d. 34
   e. 35

37. (-3, 2)
   a. 24
   b. 25
   c. 26
   d. 27
   e. 28

38. (0, -2)
   a. 31
   b. 32
   c. 33
   d. 34
   e. 35

39. (2, 0)
   a. 19
   b. 20
   c. 21
   d. 22
   e. 23

40. (0, 0)
    a. 18
    b. 19
    c. 20
    d. 21
    e. 22

41. (2, 1)
    a. 49
    b. 50
    c. 51
    d. 52
    e. 53

42. (-3, -1)
    a. 28
    b. 29
    c. 30
    d. 31
    e. 32

43. (-2, -2)
    a. 31
    b. 32
    c. 33
    d. 34
    e. 35

The following table is to be used for Questions 44-55:

Y v X >	-3	-2	-1	0	1	2	3
3	4	5	6	7	8	9	10
2	12	13	14	15	16	17	18
1	2	3	4	5	6	7	8
0	20	21	22	23	24	25	26
-1	9	10	11	12	13	14	15
-2	1	2	3	4	5	6	7
-3	6	7	8	9	10	11	12

44. (2, 2)
   a. 14
   b. 15
   c. 16
   d. 17
   e. 18

45. (-3, 3)
   a. 3
   b. 4
   c. 5
   d. 6
   e. 7

46. (0, 1)
   a. 1
   b. 2
   c. 3
   d. 4
   e. 5

47. (-3, -3)
   a. 6
   b. 7
   c. 8
   d. 9
   e. 10

48. (1, 1)
   a. 4
   b. 5
   c. 6
   d. 7
   e. 8

49. (3, 1)
   a. 4
   b. 5
   c. 6
   d. 7
   e. 8

50. (-2, 0)
   a. 20
   b. 21
   c. 22
   d. 23
   e. 24

51. (1, -3)
   a. 8
   b. 9
   c. 10
   d. 11
   e. 12

52. (2, 2)
   a. 14
   b. 15
   c. 16
   d. 17
   e. 18

53. (-3, 0)
   a. 18
   b. 19
   c. 20
   d. 21
   e. 22

54. (-2, 0)
   a. 19
   b. 20
   c. 21
   d. 22
   e. 23

55. (-3, 2)
   a. 10
   b. 11
   c. 12
   d. 13
   e. 14

The following table is to be used for Questions 56-70:

Y v X >	-3	-2	-1	0	1	2	3
3	2	3	4	5	6	7	8
2	3	4	5	6	7	8	9
1	0	1	2	3	4	5	6
0	-3	-2	-1	0	1	2	3
-1	-6	-5	-4	-3	-2	-1	0
-2	4	5	6	7	8	9	10
-3	-2	-1	0	1	2	3	4

56. (0, 2)
   a. 4
   b. 5
   c. 6
   d. 7
   e. 8

57. (2, 3)
   a. 4
   b. 5
   c. 6
   d. 7
   e. 8

58. (0, 0)
   a. -3
   b. -2
   c. -1
   d. 0
   e. 1

59. (1, -2)
   a. 6
   b. 7
   c. 8
   d. 9
   e. 10

60. (-3, -2)
   a. 4
   b. 5
   c. 6
   d. 7
   e. 8

61. (3, 1)
   a. 6
   b. 7
   c. 8
   d. 9
   e. 10

62. (1, 1)
   a. 0
   b. 1
   c. 2
   d. 3
   e. 4

63. (2, 2)
   a. 5
   b. 6
   c. 7
   d. 8
   e. 9

64. (-1, -1)
   a. -6
   b. -5
   c. -4
   d. -3
   e. -2

65. (-2, 2)
   a. 3
   b. 4
   c. 5
   d. 6
   e. 7

66. (1, 0)
   a. -2
   b. -1
   c. 0
   d. 1
   e. 2

67. (-3, 0)
   a. -5
   b. -4
   c. -3
   d. -2
   e. -1

68. (-2, 2)
   a. 3
   b. 4
   c. 5
   d. 6
   e. 7

69. (2, 2)
   a. 4
   b. 5
   c. 6
   d. 7
   e. 8

70. (0, 2)
   a. 6
   b. 7
   c. 8
   d. 9
   e. 10

Answers on Reading Tables

1. d.
2. b.
3. a.
4. c.
5. a.
6. c.
7. c.
8. b.
9. b.
10. d.
11. d.
12. b.
13. d.
14. e.
15. b.
16. e.
17. e.
18. c.
19. a.
20. b.
21. c.
22. e.
23. c.
24. a.
25. e.
26. d.
27. c.

28. d.

29. c.

30. d.

31. d.

32. e.

33. d.

34. b.

35. e.

36. c.

37. e.

38. d.

39. b.

40. a.

41. b.

42. a.

43. b.

44. d.

45. b.

46. e.

47. a.

48. c.

49. e.

50. b.

51. c.

52. d.

53. c.

54. c.

55. c.

56. c.

57. e.

58. d.

59. c.

60. a.

61. a.

62. e.

63. d.

64. c.

65. b.

66. d.

67. c.

68. b.

69. e.

70. a.

Chapter 14 – Instrument Comprehension

The instrument comprehension section of the AFOQT exam tests your knowledge of the instruments that you use while flying. You will use this segment to review the compass headings of a plane, degree of banking and climb or dive aspects of an airplane.

Artificial Horizon

There are two instrument dials that you should be familiar with. The first is the artificial horizon. The dial illustrates a plane's approximate with respect to the actual horizon. The black bar shows whether the plane is flying true, banking to the left or right, climbing or descending.

Using the yoke, a pilot can make corrections using the yoke to level out a plane or monitor a change in attitude as necessary—turn right, left, an ascent above the horizon or a descent below. It is important to make attitude changes very gently as sudden, violent or drastic changes can cause the plane to stop flying and go into a stall or dive.

Compass Readings

The compass indicates the direction the plane is traveling. The arrow points upward when you are heading north. Let's look at two examples of how a compass would be read. The first shows the plane heading north, while the second shows the plane heading west.

Question

To answer each question:

1. Read the information indicated by the artificial horizon. Look at how the plane is flying. Does it indicate a straight and level path, is the plane banking to the left or right, is it gaining altitude (above the horizon line) or losing altitude (below the horizon line)?

2. Check the direction of travel according to the compass heading.

3. Look at the four silhouettes that appear on the screen. These show if the plane is heading east— pointing to the right—or heading west, pointing left.

The instrument comprehension test will require you to study the compass and the artificial horizon carefully. Understanding how a plane is flying and where it is heading is vital.

Chapter 15 – Block Counting

The block-counting section of the AFOQT test identifies your assess how a series of blocks are arranged. The subtest focuses on your spatial knowledge and your logical reasoning skills.

In addition to working with detailed images, you will be tested on recall. You will see the same image for several of the questions and be required to recall as much information as you can about it.

You will spend 8 to 10 seconds on each question on average.

The Test Explained

The following steps should be consistent throughout the entire test:

1. You will be presented with an image featuring a series of blocks all arranged in one large mass that can vary in shape. However, the blocks should be consistent in size.

The blocks will be displayed on the screen in one shape. This will be a cube shape in most situations and the blocks will connect with one another to produce a distinct shape.

2. A few numbers will appear.

The numbers will appear on specific blocks within the larger shape. There will be one number per block. You may also find that there are a few blocks that do not have numbers. These blocks should not be discounted, as they might have an impact on the questions.

3. Review the question based on the block you have to work with.

You might be asked a question, such as how many other blocks border the one that you are reading about. You may also have to list which block is the closest to the one you are looking at.

4. Continue working with the same image for the questions that you are being asked until you are presented with something new.

You might be given 5 to 7 questions for a particular shape. There will be five answer choices for each question.

Critical Points For the Block-Counting Segment

1. You will have to review how the blocks are positioned with one another based on a three-dimensional plane.

While many of the blocks might appear to be two-dimensional, be cautious in identifying them.

2. The blocks in each shape will be the same size and all rectangular.

Operate on the assumption that all the blocks in each shape are the same size.

3. The cube shapes will not always be complete cubes.

There are times when the shapes that you review will look incomplete. Sometimes you might see a few layers where there are no blocks to be seen. Meanwhile, there might be some gaps on the top part of a shape or on a side.

4. There are no empty spaces within each shape.

Many of the blocks be unlabeled. But at the same time, those unlabeled blocks are not necessarily empty spaces. Each part of a shape will be filled with a block in some way, even if the block does not have a label.

5. You will have to recall the blocks that you have already been presented with.

You will have to recall the blocks that you have already seen and figure out from there how many blocks are in the shape.

6. Be willing to count twice.

Do not be fooled into thinking that your first answer is always correct. Look at the layout twice.

7. Notice the orientation of the blocks.

Some of the blocks that you will see will be oriented from left to right. Others will be vertically aligned so that they appear taller than they are wide. All of these blocks are the same length.

8. Time yourself when practicing this part of the AFOQT exam.

The extremely short window that you have for completing the block-counting segment of the AFOQT exam makes it tough to complete. You should time yourself based on how many seconds it takes to answer the questions about one shape. Aim for about 8 to 10 seconds per question.

Chapter 16 – Aviation Information

This part of the AFOQT exam assesses your understanding of aviation functions. This includes looking at how an airplane works and the plane's mechanical features. The concepts tested on the aviation segment tend to be relatively basic.

The test may be easier for you to complete if you have a working knowledge of Federal Aviation Administration regulations.

This part of the guide focuses on identifying many terms involved with aerodynamics, how a plane is controlled, the technical features of airplanes, features of various types of airports and the general maintenance of planes.

Note: The following chapter focuses mainly on work with airplanes. Helicopters share many of the aspects involved with airplanes and are also covered on this portion of the AFOQT exam. However, the mechanisms and features of a helicopter are different and will be discussed in a separate chapter.

The 4 Aspects of Aerodynamics

Aerodynamics is a concept that refers to how a plane moves in the air. Mastering the four aspects of aerodynamics is critical to successfully flying a plane.

1. Lift

Lift allows the plane to stay in the air and get beyond the force of gravity. When the plane is moving forward, airflow passes over the surface of the wing. The wings are shaped to allow airflow to travel faster over the top wing surface than the bottom surface. This produces lift.

2. Drag

Drag is a force that hinders the ability of a plane to move. The air that flows toward a plane produces the greatest drag. This force against the body of the plane requires the plane to use more power in order to compensate. Drag must be countered by a thrust that is equal or greater in value.

3. Thrust

Thrust is produced when an aircraft is being propelled through the air. There must be enough thrust to overcome drag. An airplane's engines are responsible for producing the thrust. While the physical design of the plane may also help with reducing drag, it's the thrust that will make the biggest impact.

4. Airfoil

An airfoil is a cross-section of the wing of a plane. The upper surface is concave while the underside is not. When in motion, air travels faster over the upper surface than the underside, causing a difference in air pressure between the air over the wing and the air under the wing, which produces lift.

The angle of the airfoil to the base (underside of the wing) is known as the angle of attack. This is the distance between the flow direction and the chord line, which is a line from the airfoil's front to back .

The critical angle is the angle of attack that creates the best lift possible. The value will vary based on how fast the aircraft is, how dense the air is and the angle of attack. If the angle of attack decreases so that the speed of airflow over the top of the wing is equal to or less than the speed of the air under the wing, the plane will stop flying and stall.

Types of Motion

Controlling the plane requires knowledge of the plane's center of gravity.

1. Roll

A roll is a rotation of an aircraft on a longitudinal axis from front to back. A roll develops when the lift changes between wings. This happens when one wing is dropped and has less lift than the other wing. This action allows the pilot to steer the plane from left to right.

2. Banking

Banking is a form of rolling where the steering of the plane is more pronounced. Ailerons—hinged surfaces on the trailing edges of the wings—are used in banking. These help control the general lateral balance of the plane.

3. Yaw

The yaw is the rotation on the plane's vertical axis. This directly influences the direction that a plane travels. The nose of the aircraft is controlled by the rudder control pedals. These keep the plane heading in the right direction alongside the roll, helping steer the plane.

4. Pitch

The pitch is the angle the plane is in by tilting the nose up or down. The nose can be tilted upward to help the aircraft climb when the plane needs more propulsion to overcome drag and keep the speed the same as when flying level. The nose can be tilted down to support the gradual, gentle descent of the plane.

5. Stall

A plane stalls when it experiences a drop in lift and an elevated amount of drag. The plane's nose is in an upward altitude and, in actuality, the plane is no longer flying. It seems to "mush" in the air. To exit a stall, the pilot reduces the angle of attack by dropping the nose and increasing the speed so that the correct amount of air is flowing over the wings to allow the plane to fly once more. The engines and other features in the plane remain functional while in a stall.

6. Spin

If a pilot does not correct a stall properly, the plane will start to go into a spin, which is an issue where one wing drops radically so that only one wing is actually flying. The spin starts with the incipient stage, which is where the spinning starts to occur after a stall. Without correction, the spin fully develops as the plane starts to enter a near-vertical spiral. A flat spin is when the plane remains parallel to the ground and spins around its center of gravity. This is the most dangerous kind of spin because if left uncorrected, the plane will "pancake" on the ground.

Controls and Control Surfaces

The controls are what the pilot uses from within the cockpit to adjust or change attitude.

1. Rudder

The rudder is the flight-control mechanism on the tail of the plane. It's responsible for keeping the plane stable. The rudder controls the yaw and keeps the opposing yaw, created by the ailerons, from interfering.

2. Ailerons

The ailerons are small hinged sections on the trailing edge of each wing used to create a rolling motion. The ailerons control the roll of the plane and eventually, its lateral balance. When the right aileron is set up, the aircraft rolls to the right, and vice versa for a roll to the left. The wing that rises up experiences an increased lift and drag, while the aircraft yaws in the direction of the raised wing.

3. Elevators

An elevator is a material on the tail wing that controls the pitch, which refers to the position of the nose whether it is pointing up or down from the rest of the plane. The nose can be tilted down through the elevator to increase the lift, but this will cause the plane to lower in altitude. The nose can also be tilted upwards through the elevator to increase elevation, although that results in a reduced lift and in a slightly reduced speed as the plane attempts to rise high enough to cover the change in the pitch.

4. Flaps

Flaps are hinged sections on the trailing edge of each wing. When activated (dropped), they cause the plane to fly at a slower speed without stalling.

Propulsion

Propulsion, created by an engine, allows a plane to move forward on the ground or in the air. An engine connected to a propeller is used on smaller aircraft. The propeller spins to increase the airflow over the wings.

A rocket engine is used for larger planes. An engine mixes fuel with oxidizers in a combustion chamber. The heat exhaust is released to help propel the jet. This is useful when wanting to travel faster or when the aircraft has a heavy load.

A gas turbine engine or jet engine is also used with particular airplanes. Fuel and air are combined in a combustion chamber from which heat exhaust is then released, similar to a rocket engine. A gas turbine engine may not be as powerful as a jet engine.

Mach Speeds

The speed of a plane is measured in miles per hour in many situations, but Mach speeds can be used to figure out how fast a plane is going versus the speed of sound. Speed of sound is measured as Mach 1, which is 767.269 miles per hour. A sonic boom develops when the aircraft reaches Mach 1.

Mach speeds are measured in the following ways:

1. Subsonic (Mach 0.8 or lower, under 609 mph)

Subsonic speed is similar to a traditional passenger airplane. The speed is produced by propulsion and a plane's general ability to overcome drag. Many subsonic planes are large commercial or cargo planes that have extreme weight.

2. Transonic (Mach 0.8 to 1.3, up to 914 mph)

A transonic plane needs swept wings in order for it to attain a sonic boom. A swept wing has an angle that goes backward from its root instead of going sideways. This wing helps keep a shock wave from developing while controlling the plane.

3. Supersonic (Mach 1.3 to 5, 915 to 3,806 mph)

A supersonic jet needs firm and sharp edges. The airfoil sections must also be narrow enough to keep a dramatic amount of drag from developing, thus making it harder to control the plane. The SR-71 Blackbird and Concorde are good examples of planes that can handle supersonic speeds.

4. Hypersonic (Mach 5 to 10, 3,806 to 7,680 mph)

The skin of the plane needs to be drastically cooled and made with a material such as nickel-titanium. The wings are smaller in size to allow the plane to move faster. A reduced body area decreases drag. The X-15 is listed as the fastest plane to have ever traveled, as this hypersonic jet can attain speeds of Mach 6.7 or 4,520 mph.

5. High-Hypersonic (Mach 10 to 25, 7,680 to 19,031 mph)

A high-hypersonic plane travels at extremely fast speeds and, due to the silicate tiles used in its construction, is capable of enduring intense heat. As a result, high-hypersonic planes are used only for space exploration. The NASA X-43A is one such example, attaining speeds of Mach 9.6 or 7,365 mph. For safety's sake, such jets must be unmanned.

6. Reentry (Mach 25 or greater)

The reentry point happens when a plane leaves the planet's atmosphere and escapes gravitational pull. The plane has an ablative heat shield that is capable of managing the intense heat produced. This occurs mainly among aeronautical planes that are controlled by NASA.

Fuselage

The fuselage is the main body of the plane that carries people and cargo. The cockpit, which is where the controls of the plane are located, is a critical part of the fuselage.

The goal when engineering fuselage is to ensure the aircraft can handle the intense stress of air travel. The fuselage is designed to accommodate the bending that occurs when force is applied to the body of the plane and compression that causes materials to shrink.

The fuselage requires a truss. This is a rigid frame that supports the compression and tension produced by flight. The beams, struts and other truss features are firm enough to create a body that will keep the plane moving without being restrictive.

The monocoque design of a truss is a single-shell frame that increases the strength of the skin. The frame uses formers that dictate the shape of the fuselage. A semi-monocoque design may also be used as a hybrid option for the fuselage.

The fuselage also has a few additional features that will support its body:

1. Boom

A boom is found on the end of the fuselage and includes the fuel tanks. It extends the tail wing outward to provide stable control for the plane. In most cases, there are two booms on a plane. This is to support enough fuel and ensure the aircraft is easy to control and there are no risks involved with keeping the plane upright and manageable.

2. Nacelle

The nacelle is a compartment that goes on the fuselage or inside the wings. Nacelles keep the engine separate from the cockpit and the landing gear. Nacelles protect the rest of the plane and reduce any possible risks during operation.

3. Cowling

The cowling of a plane is the panel that covers the aircraft engine. The cowling can be removed as a means of gaining direct access to the engine for maintenance purposes. The cowling should allow air to flow into the engine, preventing overheating.

4. Fairings

A fairing secures the spaces in between many components inside a plane. The fairing works on a wing tip, rudder or aileron flap among other features. Fairings keep a plane from experiencing too much drag. This in turn makes the engine more effective and may result in a reduced amount of fuel usage.

5. Landing Gear

The landing gear is the wheels, struts and any cable connections of the plane. These are all under the fuselage. There are planes that have a nose wheel and two main wheels. For many heavy planes, there are a series of wheels in tandem. Some landing gear is retractable.

Wings

The wings produce the lift needed to propel the plane off the ground and keep the plane in the air. The shape of the wings influences the lift and balance of the plane.

The way the wings are attached to the fuselage will influence the performance of the plane. The more common positions include:

1. A low wing features the wings on the bottom part of the fuselage.

2. A mid wing is in the middle of the fuselage.

3. The high wing is attached to the top of the fuselage.

4. A dihedral wing can be attached to the top or bottom of the fuselage, angled either up or down. The wings are neither straight nor horizontal in this situation.

5. A gull wing is bent upward toward the wing root. This wing may also appear on the top or bottom of the fuselage.

6. An inverted gull has the wing bent downward toward the wing root. This can also appear on the top or bottom of the fuselage.

Regardless of the style, a series of wing spars is required to keep the wing stable. A wing spar supports the fuselage and engines. The skin on the wing will be fiberglass, wood or aluminum.

A cantilevered design may be used to keep drag down. A braced design features external supports or rigid struts. Some wires may also be used to produce tension.

Completing Flight Maneuvers

There are four main flight maneuvers:

1. Ascend

In order to make the nose or pitch of the plane have an ascending attitude, pull back on the control column to activate the elevator. The nose will move upward, thus allowing the plane to rise.

2. Descend

Push forward on the control column and the nose will point downward. All changes in attitude should be performed gently as you do not want the plane to stop flying or to go into a dive.

3. Roll

A roll occurs when either wing is lower than the other. Turning the control column to the right will decrease the airflow of the right wing, causing it to drop or tilt to the right, and will start a roll to the right. The aileron will rise up on the right wing causing the plane to turn right. It is critical to maintain air speed while in the turn or a plane will lose altitude.

4. Yaw

The yaw or turn action happens when the plane moves on its vertical axis but does not affect the attitude of the wings. Added pressure on the right and left rudder pedal will respectively cause a yaw to the right and left. A yaw is a very gentle turn without decreasing the airflow over the wings and neither wing will drop or tilt the plane.

Controlled Flight

When going long distances, you will need to get the plane flying in the desired heading at the designated altitude. The key is to ensure the plane is level with the horizon, and that speed and altitude are constant. At the point the plane is flying straight and level, the pilot will use a trim wheel to adjust the plane's center of gravity. This allows the pilot to use almost no pressure on the control column.

Turns

Added pressure on the aileron will lower a wing to facilitate a turn. The distance involved in turning has to be mentally calculated so as to allow enough time for the full maneuver.

The three types of turns are:

1. Shallow – a bank of less than 20 degrees

2. Medium – a bank of between 20 and 45 degrees

3. Steep – a bank greater than 45 degrees

The steep turn has the fastest results, but it also produces the greatest pressure and risk to the plane and cargo. Shallow turns, executed gently, are always recommended.

Climbing and Descending

Climbing and descending respectively increase and lessen a plane's elevation. The pressure imposed on the elevator will dictate whether a plane goes up or down. Lowering the elevator will cause the nose to rise up, and raising the elevator causes the nose to point downward. The elevator is activated by either pulling back or pushing forward on the control column.

You will experience drag when climbing. That drag must be countered with added thrust (power).

The thrust (power) must be decreased while descending. As you descend, the plane will start to naturally experience a faster speed due to the lack of drag and the earth's natural gravitational pull. The drop down when you use gravity with a reduction in thrust is known as a glide. The drop in altitude and decreased power allow a plane to gently descend.

The Flight Envelope

Every plane has a flight envelope created by the manufacturer of the plane. This is the general range of how a plane can be operated safely. The envelope indicates the horsepower of the engine(s) and the horsepower needed for the plane to stay level and maintain a constant speed. It includes maximum speeds, fuel capacity and the weight of cargo and passengers (including flight staff) that a plane can carry safely. It also indicates the maximum allowed for steep turns.

The envelope may be measured through a doghouse plot. This plot is a graphic measure of how much power is needed based on the speed and altitude of a plane. The measurement can reveal how fast a plane is able to travel, the Q-corner involved and the maximum altitude that a particular plane can reach.

The doghouse plot reveals that a plane can accelerate quite well, but after a while it will start to slow or stall. The energy bleed rate is a measure of the maximum altitude a plane can reach and still fly with constant speed.

Knowing the Airport, the Rules and Air Traffic Control

All pilots have the responsibility to know the airport they intend to leave from or arrive at.

Unless the airport is listed as unmanned, the pilot will be expected to contact Air Traffic Control, otherwise known as the tower, well out from the airport. A pilot will then receive instructions pertaining to the altitude that should be used to approach the airport and the required heading. This allows the tower to keep planes at different elevations to avoid collisions. The tower will tell the pilot when to enter a pattern for landing at a particular runway and when it is safe to turn on final. Final is the path directly to the runway. The tower will indicate the plane's call letters and say "clear to land." After landing, the tower will tell the pilot which exit to take to get safely off the runway. The reverse order is used when a pilot wants to enter a runway to prepare for takeoff. He has to first contact the tower, tell the tower his intentions and wait for instructions. The tower will tell the pilot what entry to use (designated by letters), what runway and when he is cleared for takeoff.

The tower will also give the pilot instructions on where to taxi the plane and park.

Runway Lights

A series of runway lights will be activated to ensure that the pilot can see the location and attitude of the runway. Such lights are vital for evening flights and for when a plane needs to land when the visibility may be compromised. There are multiple types of runway lights:

1. Identifier lights – These are flashing lights that appear at the ends of the runway.

2. End lights – There are four lights on the two ends of the runway. These indicate the position of the runway. They will appear green from the sky and red when the plane is on the runway.

3. Edge lights – These are white lights along each side of the runway.

4. Centerline lights – The lights for the centerline appear in the middle of the runway between the edge lights. The lights are bright and white and w appear every 50 feet. The lights change to white and red for the last 3,000 feet of the runway. Those lights will be red near the end, warning that the plane is nearing the end of the runway and must stop.

5. Touchdown zone lights – The zone lights are white bars that appear on the sides of the centerline. These should be visible for about 3,000 feet to illustrate the best possible place for the plane to land or touchdown.

6. Taxiway centerline lead lights – There are green and yellow lead-off and lead-on lights that mark where traffic is to move. This is to dictate which plane has access to a runway.

7. Land and hold short lights – These lights are white and blink often. They designate when a plane needs to hold short of the runway.

8. Approach lights – A series of strobe lights illustrate the beginning of the runway. The plane can be landed safely any place beyond the strobes.

The control tower will trigger the lights to help a pilot land properly. Every pilot is required to be able to distinguish between these lights based on their colors, how often they are blinking and any unusual features of the particular airport.

Maintaining an Airplane at an Airport

Most airports have facilities to provide maintenance for a plane, a designated area to load passengers and cargo, fueling facilities and parking areas.

There should be hangars designated to different companies that provide maintenance and repair services.

History of Aviation

You could be asked questions in the AFOQT exam about the history of aviation.

Here are some basic facts on aviation history:

1. The modern helicopter was inspired by Leonardo da Vinci designs in 1485. The ornithopher is considered to be the basis of the modern helicopter.

2. Lighter-than-air aviation focuses on moving forward and overcoming drag. The development of the hot-air balloon in the eighteenth century was particularly important to the advent of air travel.

3. The fixed-wing aircraft was introduced in 1799 by Sir George Cayley. The design required a person to use body motions to steer a plane launched from a high elevation. There was no propulsion, unlike modern aviation devices.

4. The development of engines to create thrust ensured a plane could take off from the ground. The designs of Otto Lilienthal in the nineteenth century allowed planes to travel long distances in the air.

5. In 1903, Orville and Wilbur Wright successfully achieved flight.

6. World War I particularly influenced the further development of airplanes.

7. The jet engine was developed in the 1950s as a means of making air travel easier and faster.

8. Air travel has now become more common in society than ever before.

The evolution of the aviation industry suggests that there is no limit as to what may happen in the field in the future. Those who are in the Air Force may witness new developments in aviation firsthand.

Chapter 17 – Helicopter

Many people in the Air Force are taught to fly helicopters instead of traditional planes. The design of the helicopter is significantly different from a plane. Therefore, a helicopter can do things that a fixed-wing aircraft cannot.

Rotor Blade Controls

The rotor blades on top of a helicopter are responsible for producing the lift needed to keep the helicopter in the air. Another set of blades on the end of the helicopter provide balance.

The speed of the rotor is measured in rotor rotations per minute or rpm. A faster rpm will produce more lift. Reducing the speed allows a helicopter to descend.

A helicopter has a series of levers for improved control. Cyclic and collective pitch levers are used to adjust the overall pitch. The cyclic lever controls the side to side and forward to backward motions on a helicopter. The collective lever adjusts up and down motions as it increases or decreases the pitch of the blades.

A helicopter also has foot controls to adjust the direction that the tail rotor is spinning. The right pedal turns the helicopter's nose right and the tail left. The left pedal moves the nose left and the tail right.

Swash Plate Assembly

The swash plate assembly on a helicopter is an instrument that receives input from the flight controls and conveys it to the rotor blades. The upper plate links to the rotor mast and rotates to convey information from the controls to the rotor blades. The lower plate stays fixed in place and supports a series of ball bearings that allow the upper plate to move and influence the motions of the helicopter.

Stabilization

The helicopter needs to be kept stable so it will be safe to pilot and easy to control. A stabilizer bar (also known as a flybar) is used for this purpose. The bar helps produce a consistent amount of rotation and reduces vibrations caused by the rotor blades.

Transmission and Power

A helicopter is powered by an engine and a separate transmission. The engine propels the helicopter by activating the blades and influencing how fast they rotate. A gas turbine engine is the most common type of engine used in helicopters. The turbine engine produces enough thrust to get a helicopter off the ground. More importantly, the engine ensures that a helicopter maintains a consistent speed.

The engine is supported by a transmission. The transmission transfers power and speed to the rotors. A rotor mast links to the top end of the transmission. This is the shaft that the blades spin around.

Landing

Landing skids on the underside of the helicopter are flat and provide support to the entire weight of the helicopter, including its engine, transmission, blades and fuselage. The skids are lightweight and less expensive than wheels.

The general motion of the helicopter has to be decreased to land properly without causing any damage. The landing skids are not retractable and do not cause significant drag.

Some larger helicopters have wheels as landing gear. These are for cases where a helicopter is going to transport a massive amount of weight.

Aviation Information Questions

1. What is a truss on an airplane fuselage?
   a. Steel tubing
   b. Wood paneling
   c. Base floor
   d. Design control
   e. Link to a propeller

2. What makes up the fuselage of the airplane?
   a. Cabin
   b. Cargo area
   c. Cockpit
   d. Landing gear
   e. All of the above

3. A biplane is named because it has two_____.
   a. Engines
   b. Wing sets
   c. Landing wheels
   d. Propellers
   e. Cockpit seats

4. What happens with regards to the ailerons on a plane when the aircraft rolls to the left?
   a. The left aileron goes up
   b. The left aileron goes down
   c. The right aileron remains steady
   d. The right aileron moves in the same direction as the left one
   e. Nothing happens to the ailerons when turning

5. What can be done when the boom on a plane is a little larger?
   a. Add more passengers
   b. Incorporate a larger engine
   c. Add a new propeller
   d. Produce a housing for the landing gear
   e. Any of these options may work

6. Which form of stress is not necessarily important to consider when looking at the way the fuselage of a plane is built?
    a. Torsion
    b. Shear
    c. Bending
    d. Condensation
    e. Tension

7. Oxidizers are needed for this type of engine:
    a. Rocket
    b. Propeller
    c. Gas turbine
    d. Jet
    e. All of the above

8. What happens when a plane is spinning around its own center of gravity?
    a. Flat spin
    b. Fully developed spin
    c. Incipient spin
    d. Regular spin
    e. There is no real chance this could happen

9. The yaw is the rotation on what axis?
    a. Horizontal
    b. Lateral
    c. Diagonal
    d. Vertical
    e. None of the above

10. What should you do in the event that the plane stalls?
    a. Slow down the plane
    b. Reduce the angle of attack
    c. Turn in a different direction
    d. Deploy the landing gear
    e. Allow the ailerons to protrude

11. What can the wing skin be made of?
    a. Wood
    b. Aluminum
    c. Carbon fiber
    d. Fiberglass
    e. All of the above

12. What should you do to reduce the pitch?
    a. Lower the elevator
    b. Raise the elevator
    c. Add pressure to the aileron
    d. Add pressure to the rudder
    e. Reduce the engine power

13. What should be done to reduce the intensity of the drag when the plane is climbing?
    a. Apply a slight roll
    b. Reduce the pressure added to the elevator
    c. Increase the thrust
    d. Complete a steep turn
    e. Add more power to the rudder panel

14. A shallow turn would be a bank of how many degrees?
    a. 15
    b. 25
    c. 30
    d. 35
    e. 45

15. What is the smallest possible steep turn based on the degrees from the bank?
    a. 38
    b. 42
    c. 46
    d. 50
    e. 54

16. If the aircraft needs 600 horsepower for it to maintain a stable and level flight and the engine can produce 1000 horsepower, what is the extra power rating?
    a. 300
    b. 400
    c. 500
    d. 600
    e. 700

17. The highest line on a doghouse plot on the y-axis would be:
    a. Maximum altitude
    b. When you would stall
    c. Your top speed
    d. A and B
    e. A and C

18. What is the furthest measurement on the X-axis on the doghouse plot?
    a. The top speed that you could travel in your plane
    b. The rate of acceleration on a plane
    c. How fast you can travel based on altitude
    d. A and B
    e. A and C

19. The tarmac at an airport is suitable for the following activity:
    a. Refueling
    b. Loading and unloading passengers and cargo
    c. Extensive repairs
    d. Long-term storage
    e. A and B

20. A plane must support a particular speed to move forward. The minimum speed that is required to sustain a safe flight is:
    a. Dive speed
    b. Cruise speed
    c. Stall speed
    d. Motor speed
    e. Q-rate speed

21. How can you distinguish the edge lights on the runway?
    a. They appear on the lengths of the runway
    b. These are on the front and end parts of the runway
    c. The lights are bright red
    d. The lights produce a strobe effect
    e. The lights may not be active at all times

22. What can be noticed about the runway centerline light system when the plane is near the end of the runway?
    a. The lights start to turn red
    b. You will notice intense flashing effects
    c. The lights will emit sirens
    d. The lights may spread around the surface of the runway
    e. Nothing special may be noted

23. What is the difference between the words terminal and concourse at an airport?
    a. The terminal is only for planes
    b. The concourse is for housing people
    c. The terminal requires exclusive access
    d. The concourse is the only place that requires safety work
    e. No real difference

24. What will limit the flight of a plane?
    a. Drag
    b. Lift
    c. Weight
    d. Power
    e. Thrust

25. What happens when an aircraft is banked?
    a. Stall
    b. Spin
    c. Yaw
    d. Roll
    e. Pitch

26. The body of the fuselage may potentially stretch due to which type of stress that is encountered when the plane is flying?
    a. Bending
    b. Shear
    c. Torque
    d. Tension
    e. Compression

27. A force may run parallel to a plane and cause layers of the plane to break off if the plane is not built properly or the force is too intense. This concern is known as:
    a. Bending
    b. Shear
    c. Torque
    d. Tension
    e. Compression

28. What part of the flight control links directly to the horizontal stabilizer?
    a. Elevator
    b. Aileron
    c. Rudder
    d. Boom
    e. Wing

29. To steer a helicopter, what part of the motion has to be adjusted?
    a. Rotor
    b. Pitch
    c. Spin
    d. Roll
    e. Yaw

30. Which part of the Air Traffic Control team at an airport will assist in directing a pilot toward the runway for landing?
    a. Radar
    b. Local
    c. Ground
    d. Departure
    e. Approach

31. The local control at an Air Traffic Control station at an airport will assist in:
    a. Reviewing other flights
    b. Managing ground communication
    c. Directing movements to the apron
    d. Handling landing approaches
    e. Managing other people in the terminal

32. The main key of the doghouse plot is to show:
    a. How often the plane has been used
    b. The flight envelope
    c. How well certain maneuvers may be utilized in the air
    d. Motion effects in the plane
    e. The maximum performance standards of the plane

33. The bulkhead on the fuselage acts to:
    a. Insulate the inside of the fuselage
    b. Secure the gas tanks
    c. Resist pressure
    d. Produce a thorough body
    e. Anchor windows

34. What is the most noticeable thing when a plane stalls?
    a. The aircraft's elevation drops
    b. The speed of the aircraft slows
    c. The aircraft's wings become harder to control
    d. You start to pivot in one direction
    e. The engine is failing

35. What will the drag do to a plane?
    a. Limit its motion
    b. Resist motion
    c. Keep the plane in the air
    d. Propel the plane
    e. All of the above

36. The flight data person will have to use what data?
    a. Pre-flight information
    b. Points on the plane
    c. Flight plan
    d. FAA data
    e. All of the above

37. The cyclic pitch lever in a helicopter controls the vehicle by:
    a. Tilting the angle pitch
    b. Moving the pitch up and down
    c. Adjusting the elevation of the helicopter
    d. Changing the rotor speed
    e. Checking on the angles that the landing gear is positioned at

38. Are wheels required on a helicopter for landing?
    a. Needed for faster helicopters
    b. Depends on the size of the helicopter
    c. Always
    d. Not at all
    e. Can be switched out with landing skids

39. What happens in a climb?
    a. The plane goes faster
    b. The pressure level increases
    c. Drag increases
    d. The landing gear moves up
    e. The plane rises in altitude

40. What can be done to make up for any unintentional roll while in the air?
    a. Reduce the speed of the engine
    b. Allow the landing gear to add extra weight and pressure to level out the plane
    c. Move downward in elevation
    d. Add pressure to the ailerons in the direction that you need to correct the movement in
    e. The elevator should be positioned

41. The purpose of the cowling is to:
    a. Cover an engine
    b. Allow air to move in to an engine
    c. Store fuel
    d. A and B
    e. All of the above

42. An inverted gull wing features:
    a. A bend downward near the wing root
    b. A link in the middle part of the fuselage
    c. An upward bend
    d. A straight body
    e. An angular look

43. What makes a low, mid, or high wing similar to one another?
    a. Each wing is in the middle part of the fuselage
    b. The wing is straight in layout
    c. An angled position may be noticed
    d. The wings are bent downward
    e. Each wing is on the top part of the fuselage

44. What does compression do to an object in flight:
    a. Reduce its size
    b. Bend the item
    c. Produce a stretching motion
    d. Cause items to break off
    e. Twist the object

45. For a propeller on a plane powered by a propeller engine to work, a piston has to be activated to move a crankshaft that spins the propeller. What is needed to make this happen?
    a. Fuel needs to mix with air
    b. Fuel has to burn
    c. Heated gas is to be released
    d. A and C
    e. All 3

46. A plane is starting to spin after stalling. What is this called?
    a. Incipient
    b. Flat spin
    c. Fully developed
    d. Twisting
    e. None of the above

47. A plane moving at Mach 3.5 is moving at what speed:
    a. Transonic
    b. Re-entry speed
    c. Supersonic
    d. Hypersonic
    e. Subsonic

48. An angle of attack that will create the most lift is:
    a. Evolutionary
    b. Essential
    c. Designated
    d. Arranged
    e. Critical

49. What can influence the drag on the plane the most?
    a. Wind speed
    b. Airfoil
    c. Weight
    d. Lift
    e. Thrust

50. Lift is responsible for:
    a. Helping the plane to steer
    b. Moving the plane faster
    c. Allowing a plane to stay in the air
    d. Controlling the general speed of the plane in real time
    e. Ensuring the plane does not wear out

51. The drag that occurs from the rear of a plane can be opposed by:
    a. Compression
    b. Tension
    c. Weight
    d. Lift
    e. Thrust

52. Where is the cowling?
    a. On your landing gear
    b. On the tail
    c. On the wing
    d. In the fuselage
    e. Near the engine

53. What color are the edge lights on a runway?
    a. Blue
    b. Yellow
    c. White
    d. Red
    e. Green

54. The angle that is produced by the airfoil chord and the direction of the wind is the:
    a. Critical angle of attack
    b. Angle of attack
    c. Pitch angle
    d. Stall parameter
    e. Angle of incidence

55. A firewall is designed in an engine compartment to:
    a. Promote heat
    b. Prevent fires from spreading
    c. Reduce heat
    d. Establish control
    e. All of the above

56. On a biplane, the 2 sets of wings are stacked:
    a. Horizontally
    b. Vertically
    c. Diagonally
    d. They are actually retractable
    e. Any of these can work

57. According to Beroulli's Principle, an increase in speed will result in what change in pressure?
    a. Increase
    b. Decrease
    c. Expansion
    d. Change in rate
    e. No distinct change

58. A low-speed airplane will have what type of airfoil?
    a. A thick model
    b. One that covers more physical space
    c. A thin layout
    d. A lack of heat
    e. The airfoil can appear in any form in this case

59. The wingspan is the distance between:
    a. The ends of the truss
    b. The end of the wing to the root part
    c. The end of one wing to the end of the other
    d. The front and back parts of the wing
    e. The wing and its truss

60. The chord is the distance from the leading edge of a wing to:
    a. The base on the truss
    b. The central part of the wind
    c. The highest elevation on the wing
    d. Its deeper point
    e. Its trailing edge

61. How many wheels are on the landing gear of a typical plane?
    a. 2
    b. 3
    c. 4
    d. 5
    e. 6

62. A commercial jet has a greater wing sweep. As a result:
    a. The plane can turn fast
    b. It takes an extra bit of time to turn
    c. The lift is easier to maintain
    d. The drag is increased
    e. The drag is minimal

63. What makes a delta wing distinct?
    a. A triangular shape without any gaps is formed
    b. A triangular shape may come with a bend
    c. A singular line is formed
    d. The angle between the wings is strong
    e. The wings come with rounded edges

64. When the wings bend downward, the wing slant is:
    a. Neutral
    b. Positive
    c. Negative
    d. Tipped
    e. No defining terms

65. The pitch will influence the pull that the pilot is capable of producing. The pull in this case refers to:
    a. Brake
    b. Turn
    c. Exhaust
    d. Deployment
    e. Thrust

66. Blue edge lights designate what feature at an airport?
    a. Taxiway
    b. Runway
    c. Stopping point
    d. Air traffic center
    e. Terminal

67. The wing flaps on a plane can be extended. This will result in:
    a. Increased drag
    b. Increased lift
    c. Decreased speed
    d. Reduced turning radius
    e. A and B

68. The rudder is used for what controls on a fixed-wing aircraft?
    a. Inboard
    b. Outboard
    c. Upper
    d. Central
    e. Rear

69. The approach lighting system will feature the follow items that lead to a landing strip at an airport:
    a. Strobe lights
    b. Color-changing lights
    c. White lights
    d. Red lights
    e. All of these are included

70. Which Mach speed is the fastest?
   a. 3
   b. 4
   c. 5
   d. 6
   e. 7

71. At Mach 25, a plane would be in what state?
   a. Hypersonic
   b. Supersonic
   c. Transonic
   d. High-hypersonic
   e. Re-entry

72. When a plane is in re-entry, the following is noticed:
   a. Curved wings
   b. Wide angle
   c. Deep descent
   d. Head start on the engine's functionality
   e. Sturdy heat shield

73. The weight force is counteracted by:
   a. Drag
   b. Speed
   c. Wind
   d. Coverage
   e. Lift

74. The joystick in a plane will control the:
   a. Roll
   b. Pitch
   c. Climb
   d. Descent
   e. A and B

75. Straight wings are best for:
   a. High speeds
   b. Low speeds
   c. Strong turns
   d. Light turn radiuses
   e. Deep climbs

76. The yaw is a reference of the nose's ability to:
    a. Move up or down
    b. Point left or right
    c. Stretch long
    d. Change based on heat
    e. Change based on speed

77. A stall will be caused by:
    a. High climbing
    b. High air speed
    c. Low air speed
    d. Intense descent
    e. Lack of turning

78. It is easier for an aircraft rudder to work when the plane is:
    a. Faster
    b. Slower
    c. Higher in the air
    d. Lower in the air
    e. Newer in design

79. Cold air causes an increased:
    a. Pressure
    b. Amount of wind
    c. Density
    d. Amount of clouds
    e. No real difference between cold and warm air

80. What would make it harder for an aircraft to land?
    a. High elevation and heat
    b. High elevation and cold
    c. Low elevation and heat
    d. Low elevation and cold
    e. A landing near water

81. When a plane is making a maneuver in the air, the plane will have energy at the start of the movement. This energy is known as:
    a. Kinetic energy
    b. Reserve energy
    c. Potential energy
    d. Heat shift
    e. Temperature change

82. What will influence the ground speed of a plane?
    a. Wind
    b. Heat
    c. Rain
    d. Altitude
    e. Pressure

83. Newton's First Law may apply to aviation. By this, a body at rest will:
    a. Stay at rest until impacted
    b. Move about faster
    c. Take extra time to start up
    d. Shift on its own without restraint
    e. Heat up

84. Induced drag happens due to:
    a. Outside items near the plane
    b. Lift
    c. Shift in the way how the plane works
    d. Pressure
    e. Elevation

85. The elevator is designed to control:
    a. Pitch
    b. Angle
    c. Roll
    d. Yaw
    e. Vertical control

86. The movement on a vertical axis is known as the:
    a. Yaw
    b. Roll
    c. Angle
    d. Pitch
    e. Turn

87. A movement on a longitudinal axis is the:
    a. Roll
    b. Turn
    c. Yaw
    d. Angle
    e. Pitch

88. What feature should a heliport have to show where and how to land?
   a. A triangle
   b. A large H
   c. A box
   d. A T symbol
   e. A cross layout

89. The true altitude of a plane is the vertical distance:
   a. Above the ground
   b. Above sea level
   c. Based on pressure
   d. Based on speed
   e. Uncorrected content

90. The sea level on an altimeter on a plane refers to the height of your plane versus:
   a. The runway you went off of
   b. The tides in your area
   c. How often tides may change at a time
   d. Speeds for the plane
   e. A major body of water

91. An AH is what type of helicopter?
   a. Attack
   b. Altitude
   c. Analysis
   d. Aviary
   e. Aeronautical

92. A CH is what type of helicopter?
   a. Crew
   b. Convenience
   c. Chopper
   d. Craft
   e. Cargo

93. A KC plane is a plane designed to handle:
   a. Kinetic energy actions
   b. Speed layouts
   c. High elevation movements
   d. Shifts in air speed
   e. Aerial refueling

94. An MH is a helicopter that has been modified for:
    a. Moving objects
    b. Military actions
    c. Aerial refueling
    d. Shifting movements
    e. Changes in elevation

95. An HH helicopter is used for:
    a. Heavy lifting
    b. High elevation purposes
    c. High speeds
    d. Hard materials
    e. Hazardous material carriage

96. An electronic airplane may rely on electronic controls for:
    a. Speed
    b. Elevation
    c. Moving the plane
    d. Managing turns
    e. Planning the landing gear

97. The indicated airspeed refers to the speed:
    a. Based on the instruments in the plane
    b. Based on pressure
    c. Based on temperature
    d. In accordance with drag
    e. In accordance to mechanical risks

98. The true airspeed reflects the impact of what on speed?
    a. Compression
    b. Pressure
    c. Turning efforts
    d. Change in elevation
    e. All of the above

99. Can a helicopter with wheels as its landing gear make a vertical take-off?
    a. Yes
    b. No
    c. Depends on elevation
    d. Depends on slope
    e. Based on cargo

100.   A monoplane is distinct for having:
  a. A singular wing in the middle
  b. A large center wing
  c. A single carriage space
  d. One engine
  e. One set of wings

Aviation Information Answers

1. a. The truss is designed with steel or aluminum tubing to help with producing a secure body that is substantial.

2. e. The fuselage is the part of an airplane that features the space inside the body of the plane.

3. b. A biplane is a plane that features 2 sets of wings.

4. a. The position of the aileron will change when the aileron next to the wing that is rolling is changed. When the plane rolls right, the right aileron goes up and when it rolls left, the left aileron goes up.

5. b. The boom is designed to work at the rear fuselage. The boom may include a fuel tank or a larger engine layout that can produce more power at a time.

6. d. The fuselage should be able to handle condensation, especially as it flies in high elevation levels. The fuselage may bend.

7. a. A rocket engine requires oxidizers with fuel to work in the same combustion chamber to produce the exhaust needed for propulsion.

8. a. The flat spin occurs as a spin where the aircraft is spinning horizontally to the ground.

9. d. The yaw is the rotation of the plane on a vertical axis. The roll goes on a longitudinal axis, and the pitch rotates on the lateral axis.

10. b. The angle of attack should be checked based on the climb. You would have to lower that angle to avoid stalling.

11. e. The wing skin is designed to be rigid and to provide support to keep the stress produced by the plane from being too intense. All of the options listed are suitable choices.

12. b. Lowering the pitch moves the nose on the plane down. You would have to add forward pressure to control column to raising the elevator.

13. c. You must have enough thrust to where you can continue to move upward in the air. You can only use the thrust in this case to help with overcoming the extra drag that has come about.

14. a. A shallow turn entails the bank being less than 20 degrees. A is the only answer that would qualify as a shallow turn.

15. c. A steep turn would entail the bank being more than 45 degrees. C is the smallest possible steep turn that would qualify based on the answers listed here.

16. b. The extra power would be the surplus between the maximum energy setup on the engine versus the power that is required for the flight at hand. The extra power measurement may be utilized to determine how capable your plane is and if it can handle possibly dangerous conditions or situations where you are.

17. d. The y-axis on the doghouse plot entails the altitude that the plane can travel at. The top line would entail the highest possible altitude that you can reach, not to mention the height at which you would start stalling at.

18. e. The X-axis on the doghouse plot covers the speed of the plane. The furthest line of the X-axis will show the maximum speed that you can travel. The line may also rise up and show the same maximum speed based on the altitude. In some cases, the maximum speed may be the same regardless of the altitude at a given time.

19. e. The tarmac is also known as the apron. You can use the tarmac as a place for getting fuel and for loading and unloading things. Anything more extensive would require you to get the plane out to a hangar. You'd also have the use a hangar if you're going to keep your plane stored somewhere for a little while.

20. c. The stall speed is the speed at which you would travel when stalling. At this point, you should be able to keep on controlling the plane, although

you would have to correct yourself to control moving in the direction you want to go in.

21. a. The edge lights are on the sides of the runway and will run the length of the runway. The lights will distinguish where the runway is and where you have to go when traveling down here.

22. a. The lights will begin to appear red at the final 3,000 feet of the runway, and will eventually become completely red near the end. The lights appear to let you know when you need to stop the plane altogether.

23. e. The terms terminal and concourse are the same and have no difference.

24. c. The weight will impact your flight the most due to the mass being impacted mainly by the gravity pulls the aircraft down toward the ground. You would have to apply enough thrust to make it easier for you to overcome the weight.

25. d. The aircraft will roll in the direction that you want to move when you bank the plane. That is, you are lowering one wing to let the plane know which direction you want to get the plane to move out to.

26. d. Tension occurs when an object starts to stretch. The stretching motion may occur due to pressure changes among other threats impacting the quality of the plane. The stretching should stop when the plane reaches ground level, although you would have to be cautious here and note that the plane is capable of getting back to its original pattern without any possible wearing getting in the way.

27. b. The shearing process develops as parts of the plane are sheared off from the intense pressure involved with the flight.

28. a. The elevator connects to the horizontal stabilizer. The elevator will adjust the pitch as you fly.

29. b. The pitch levers will help with moving the helicopter in the air. The spin and yaw are used for a larger plane and are not for a smaller helicopter.

30. e. The approach control lets you know when you have to reach the runway and what you should be doing as you get to the runway for landing purposes.

31. a. The local control will check on what planes are actively leaving and arriving at the airport. This is to ensure that all planes that move in and out of the airport are planned well and that there is no traffic congestion or other threats involved with planes not moving well.

32. e. The doghouse plot shows how fast a plane may go and what particular elevation the plane may travel at.

33. c. The bulkhead is needed for helping to keep the fuselage from experiencing significant problems surrounding pressure levels. This comes as the pressure levels can become higher in intensity when you move a little further upward in the air.

34. a. The stalling occurs when you have reached the highest possible elevation at the current speed you are traveling at. You would have to increase the thrust on the plane to allow it to move a little faster.

35. b. Drag does not limit the force in the plane, but it will limit its ability to move forward as well as it should.

36. e. The flight data person will gather the data on the plane and what the pilot is going to do before leaving. The information would include the FAA data that has to be reviewed accordingly to ensure the plane's movement can be certified and the pilot is ready to move forward and go further.

37. a. The cyclic pitch lever controls the angle of the pitch, while the collective pitch lever will increase or decrease the pitch.

38. b. Wheels are recommended for a helicopter if it is large in size. In other cases, landing skids would be good enough.

39. e. While a climb is a rise in altitude, a descent involves a drop.

40. d. The proper pressure on the ailerons will help with countering any sudden instances of bending or shifting while in the air.

41. d. A cowling may be utilized to help with improving upon how well the plane's engine can stay functional and safe.

42. a. An inverted gull wing is bent down near the wing root. The wing may be on the top or bottom part of the fuselage.

43. b. Each of these 3 wings is straight and horizontal, although the position of the wing with regards to the rest of the fuselage will vary.

44. a. Compression is an action where the size is constricted. This is due to the intense pressure.

45. e. The propeller engine requires fuel to mix with air so the fuel can burn. After this, heated gas is released to move a piston that will spin a propeller.

46. a. The incipient process is the plane starting to spin when it stalls.

47. c. A supersonic plane will go from Mach 1 to 5.

48. e. The critical angle of attack will vary, but it should give the plane enough support to move upward.

49. c. The weight of the plane will directly impact the ability of the plane to function, especially as the weight will be impacted by the earth's gravitational pull. The added weight on the plane can make it harder for that plane to move forward and it will need more power.

50. c. With lift, force is applied by added power of the engine to ensure it can remain airborne.

51. b. The tension produced will have to manage the drag that is imposed on the plane.

52. e. The cowling is designed to cover the engine.

53. a. The blue lights appear at night and will reveal where the plane needs to stop on the runway.

54. b. The plane needs to be positioned so that the angle of attack makes allowances for the force of the wind.

55. b. The firewall will absorb the heat being produced by the engine.

56. b. The vertical arrangement of the wings makes it easier for the position of the plane to be adjusted while in the air.

57. b. The drop in pressure occurs as the plane becomes more powerful and the impact of the pressure is not as significant.

58. a. A thicker airfoil will require extra power for the plane to overcome when trying to move faster.

59. c. The wingspan is the total width of the plane from wing tip to wing tip.

60. e. The cord is a measure of the side of the wing and how the edge is positioned.

61. b. At least 3 wheels are needed to ensure that the plane can be handled well.

62. e. The wing sweep decreases drag.

63. a. The triangular shape of the wing allows the plane to handle faster speeds without much drag.

64. c. A negative wing slant produces a downward position.

65. e. The pull is a measure of the thrust or how the plane is going to produce enough energy to keep the plane moving forward.

66. a. The taxiway is needed for moving planes to the appropriate place for take-off.

67. e. When the wing flaps are extended, the drag and lift will be greater.

68. c. The rudder allows the plane to be controlled and stabilized.

69. a. The strobe lights give the pilot of a plane an indication of where the runway begins.

70. e. When the Mach number is higher, the plane flies faster.

71. e. The re-entry speed occurs when something moves back into the earth's atmosphere and the speed increases.

72. e. A heat shield protects the plane from extreme heat that occurs on re-entry.

73. e. The lift allows the plane to climb and stay airborne.

74. e. The movements on the joystick will control the plane's movement from left to right and up or down, thus influencing the roll and pitch.

75. b. The straight wing design can handle low speeds while flying.

76. b. The yaw is the movement of the plane left or right without dropping a wing.

77. c. A stall will occur when a plane is in an attitude where the wings are no longer producing lift and the plane stops flying.

78. a. The rudder is needed to stabilize the movement of the plane on a straight and level path in the air and to increase the roll from left to right when needed. When the plane is flying faster, the rudder is easier to manage.

79. c. A plane flies easier through cold air as the air is denser making more air move over the top surface of the wings so the plane needs less power to stay flying.

80. a. A high elevation produces more pressure. Heat can also thin the air is. These 2 factors will make it harder for the plane to stay flying unless more power is applied.

81. c. Potential energy is a reference to how the plane may move in the future. When something has added potential energy, it becomes easier for the plane to move forward.

82. a. Wind can make it harder for the plane to move from left to right while on the ground. The wind may influence how the take-off and landing is performed.

83. a. An object as rest will stay at rest until it suffers an impact.

84. b. The lift will cause the plane to slow as the plane rises into the air.

85. a. The pitch is how the plane moves up or down. The elevator is controls the pitch.

86. a. The yaw is the movement of a plane on its vertical axis.

87. a. The roll is the movement of a plane on its longitudinal axis.

88. b. The H painted on a surface indicates a landing spot for a helicopter. It could be painted on the ground or on the top flat area of a building.

89. b. The true altitude is based on sea level.

90. e. The altimeter measures the height of the plane based on sea level.

91. a. An attack helicopter is designed to support many missions where weapons are necessary to be carried onboard.

92. e. A cargo helicopter is designed to handle more weight either onboard or towed.

93. e. A KC plane can handle aerial refueling tasks, including ones where fuel has to be transferred to another plane in the air.

94. b. The MH designation is for military actions.

95. a. The HH helicopter is designed for heavy lifting and towing.

96. a. The electronic controls make it easier for the speed to be adjusted as needed.

97. a. The instruments should be noted as they indicate how the plane is flying.

98. b. Pressure levels can influence the quality of the air and increase the drag.

99. a. A vertical take-off is possible, although it would be best for the helicopter to do this when it does not have much weight.

100. e. The monoplane design allows for better control as it only has one set of wings.

Chapter 18 – The Self-Inventory

Although the self-description inventory section of the AFOQT exam is the longest and requires the most time, it is not graded. The inventory is simply assessing your personality to give the academy an idea of who you are.

The test is based on personality or adjective clusters that Lewis R. Goldberg devised including extraversion, conscientiousness, openness, emotional stability and agreeableness. These are considerations that relate to how well you get along with people, adapt to different situations and handle different concerns.

Service and team orientation are also assessed. Service orientation involves how well you can manage organizational functions and how much you are committed to the Air Force. The team-orientation aspect looks at how well you can work within a team or if you are more interested in working on your own.

When taking this subtest, be aware of the following:

1. You will be presented with a statement relating to who you are or what your interests are.

You will be presented with a list of statements that may or may not describe you. For example:

- I enjoy reading books.
- I like long walks on the beach.
- I think regularly about my finances.
- There's nothing that stops me from helping others.

2. You will be asked if you agree or disagree with statements.

The test will give five answers, as follows:

- Strongly agree

- Moderately agree

- Neither agree nor disagree

- Moderately disagree

- Strongly disagree

Since this is not going to be graded, you can be open and honest. Think of the inventory as a questionnaire where you are helping the Air Force get to know you.

Sample Questions

There are many questions in the AFOQT self-assessment segment. The section is designed to reveal your personality, interests, strengths, knowledge, reasoning powers, how you approach work and your ability to work with others.

Naturally, there are some questions that may indirectly relate to the Air Force. Here are some examples:

1. I enjoy reading books.

2. I like watching television.

3. I prefer meat for dinner.

4. I try to take a walk a few times a week.

5. I do well with interacting with my family.

6. I am willing to wait a little longer to get the things that I want.

7. I try my hardest to avoid problems with others.

8. My efforts to help people don't get in the way of my personal values.

9. I have no concerns about what I plan to do with my work.

10. Science is very interesting to me.

The most important part of all these questions is that there are no wrong answers.

Chapter 19 – Final Tips

The AFOQT exam is a complex test and it is vital to your admission into the Air Force. To make the most out of your studies, pay close attention to the following tips:

1.   Manage your time wisely.

You only have a certain amount of time for each section, as mentioned earlier. Be sure you review the timing for each subtest and have a plan in mind. Consider how much time you'll dedicate to each question. When testing, focus on your plan rather than on the clock.

2.   It's okay to guess once in a while.

You won't know the answer to every single question. It's okay to guess. You're only judged on the questions you answer correctly. Just narrow your guess down to the best possible answer within reason.

3.   Study in sections.

The chapters listed on this guide cover individual parts of the AFOQT exam. Rather than trying to cram everything all at once, study a different section every day, or spend two to three hours a day on a specific subtest.

4.   Enhance your writing skills.

Although there are no written parts of the AFOQT exam, you can still use writing skills to your advantage in the reading section of the test. Make sure you can identify text structures, main points, etc., as detailed in an earlier chapter of this guide.

What if you Fail?

There is a potential that you might fail the first time you take the AFOQT exam. If that happens, be aware that you can retest after 180 days (six months). The most recent AFOQT exam test score will be the one that counts.

Can you Skip Questions or Sections?

While you might want to skip a section of the test (or a question) that you're not fully familiar with, unfortunately, this isn't allowed.

Studying each part of the AFOQT exam is critical even if you don't necessarily plan on using all of the knowledge you're tested on. The information on the exam is universal throughout much of the Air Force.

Conclusion

The AFOQT exam is a comprehensive test that requires your utmost attention. It's a test of your skills and ability to handle different functions and activities in the Air Force. You will be tested on information from science and math to reading and flight instrumentation.

Completing the exam successfully will enable you to move forward toward your goal. Those who are chosen to enter the Air Force should feel positive about themselves, as they are one step closer to being certified pilots or Air Force members.

We wish you the best of luck on your AFOQT exam. We hope that this guide has provided you with a great idea of what to expect on the test and how to complete it. You will find that if you study carefully, the AFOQT exam will not be difficult.

Made in the USA
Monee, IL
01 December 2019